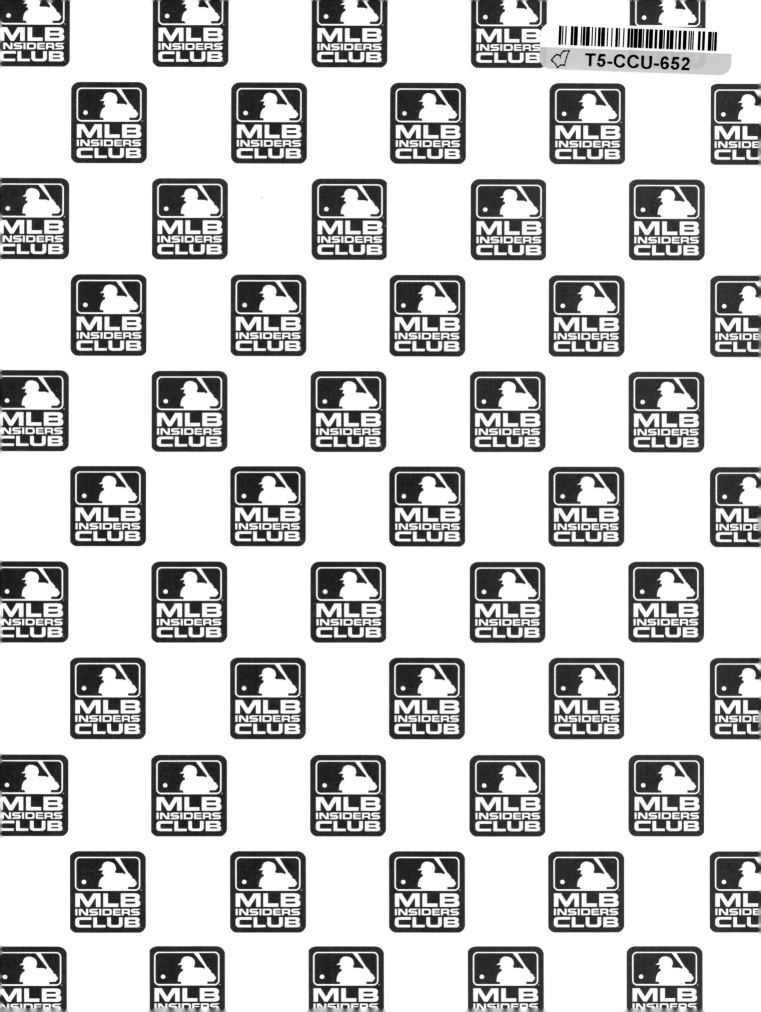

INSIDE
spring training

A behind-the-scenes look at the
Grapefruit and Cactus Leagues.

Baseball Insiders Library™

INSIDE
spring training
A behind-the-scenes look at the Grapefruit and Cactus Leagues.

MLB
INSIDERS
CLUB

Baseball Insiders Library

INSIDE SPRING TRAINING by Pete Williams
A behind-the-scenes look at the Grapefruit and Cactus Leagues.

Printed in 2010

ABOUT THE AUTHOR

Pete Williams has covered Major League Baseball and Spring Training for nearly two decades for numerous media outlets, including USA Today, The New York Times, SportsBusiness Journal *and* Fox Sports. *The author or co-author of 11 books, including* Inside the World Series *in the* Baseball Insiders Library™, *he lives with his wife and two sons in Safety Harbor, Fla., in the heart of the Grapefruit League.*

ACKNOWLEDGEMENTS

Major League Baseball would like to thank Eric Enders and Kristin Nieto for their diligent work in helping to prepare this book for publication.

MAJOR LEAGUE BASEBALL PROPERTIES

Vice President, Publishing
Donald S. Hintze

Editorial Director
Mike McCormick

Publications Art Director
Faith M. Rittenberg

Senior Production Manager
Claire Walsh

Associate Editor
Jon Schwartz

Associate Art Director
Melanie Finnern

Senior Publishing Coordinator
Anamika Chakrabarty

Project Assistant Editors
Chris Greenberg, Jodie Jordan, Jake Schwartzstein

Editorial Intern
Allison Duffy

MAJOR LEAGUE BASEBALL PHOTOS

Director
Rich Pilling

Photo Editor
Jessica Foster

MLB INSIDERS CLUB

Creative Director
Tom Carpenter

Managing Editor
Jen Weaverling

Prepress
Wendy Holdman

MLB Insiders Club
12301 Whitewater Drive
Minnetonka, MN 55343

TABLE OF CONTENTS

INTRODUCTION
8

PREGAME
10

WEEK 1
A NEW SEASON
16

WEEK 2
SHAPING UP
38

WEEK 3
FUN AND GAMES
68

WEEK 4
DIVERSIONS
92

WEEK 5
DOWN TO THE WIRE
116

WEEK 6
NORTHBOUND
140

BIBLIOGRAPHY/CREDITS
156

INDEX
157

MORNING WORKOUT
Texas Rangers players get in a stretch
during Spring Training in Florida.

INTRODUCTION

THE TRADITION OF SPRING TRAINING IN MAJOR LEAGUE BASEBALL HARKENS BACK TO A MORE innocent time, when life proceeded at a leisurely pace and baseball games were played mostly during the day. Unlike other professional sports leagues, MLB is the only one that clusters its clubs together for preseason workouts. This custom spawned the tradition of Spring Training, which has become nearly as ingrained in the sport as the World Series. The spring exhibition season, played out over a six-week period, provides a prelude to the regular season that in many respects is just as enjoyable. Nobody seems in a hurry at the start of Spring Training, unless it's to get to the beach or golf course. Aside from being a way for players and fans to ease back into the rigors of the regular season, Spring Training is the time when clubhouse chemistry is formed, torches are passed and living legends appear daily. It's when the reserved Sandy Koufax makes an annual appearance at Dodgers camp to tutor young pitchers. It's Al Kaline holding court at Tiger Town in Lakeland, Yogi Berra and Reggie Jackson working the batting cage at the Yankees' George M. Steinbrenner Field in Tampa. It's about small towns that thrive off the six weeks of attention they get from ballplayers and fans. It's the story of how former St. Petersburg mayor Al Lang built the Grapefruit League to promote Florida tourism. It's also the story of how the Cactus League flowered in Arizona, nurtured by famed baseball character Bill Veeck.

For fans back home, nothing signals the start of Spring Training more than the sight of a golf-shirt-clad local sportscaster doing a live remote as his colleagues back in the studio give him grief for having a cushy assignment. Whether it's because of greater access for autograph seekers, closer proximity to the game or the opportunity to combine baseball with a trip to the beach, world-class golf or to Disney World, Spring Training affords fans an experience far different from the regular season. Before temperatures warm in much of the country, baseball devotees look toward the upcoming campaign with a sense of hope and renewal. Each season, after all, begins with a 0-0 record and a feeling that if everything goes well, this could be the year for the home team.

Home team. It's a relative term in the spring. The residents of Vero Beach, Fla., called the Dodgers the home team longer than the folks in Los Angeles have. The Detroit Tigers have played in Lakeland, Fla., since 1934. Generations of Arizona residents have grown up fans of the Chicago Cubs and San Francisco Giants and remain loyal even a decade after the arrival of the Arizona Diamondbacks. Tampa native Fred McGriff played for six Big League teams, including the Rays, but still views the Reds as his home team, having watched them for many springs at long-gone Al Lopez Field. Almost half the franchises in the Majors have resided in their Spring Training ballparks longer than they've played in their regular-season stadiums.

Spending a day — or even a week-long vacation — at Spring Training feels like playing hooky from the responsibilities of the real world. Some fans come each year to scout their favorite teams or to get ideas for their fantasy draft, convinced they have discovered overlooked talent. Unlike years ago when Spring Training served as a time to condition bodies into game shape, today's players arrive fresh from offseason workout programs, in the best condition of the year.

The secret of Spring Training is out. MLB Network televises a full, national slate of spring games, augmenting the local coverage that has always been available. MLB.com has also made Spring Training reports easy to find and less like dispatches from exotic locales. New Spring Training complexes, especially the two-team facilities in Arizona, have transformed the experience fans enjoyed at older venues like Vero Beach, Winter Haven, Baseball City and the waterfront ballpark in downtown St. Petersburg named for Florida's own Al Lang.

Although they may change the way baseball fans experience Spring Training in the future, it's hard to find fault with such modern, fan-friendly palaces as Camelback Ranch, Surprise Stadium, Goodyear Ballpark, Roger Dean Stadium and the Peoria Sports Complex. Indeed, perhaps the biggest story of Spring Training is how it remains the quintessential baseball experience even after decades of change.

PREGAME

Although Spring Training goes back almost as far as the sport itself, 19th century baseball players would not recognize the choreographed six-week sessions that play out each year in Florida and Arizona. According to *Under the March Sun: The Story of Spring Training* by Charles Fountain, baseball clubs traveled to warm-weather destinations in the South — like New Orleans, Savannah and Charleston — to prepare for the upcoming season as far back as the 1870s. Hall of Famer Cap Anson codified Spring Training among Major League outfits when he took his Chicago White Stockings to Hot Springs, Ark., in the mid-1880s. By the late 1880s, most franchises were sending players and coaches to warmer locales for some form of preseason camp. The Washington Senators were the first to venture to Florida, training in Jacksonville in 1888.

This was not Spring Training as we think of it today, of course. Teams trained on any patch of grass they could find, and played against high school and college squads — or whatever group of local players was available. For decades, Spring Training focused on conditioning and sweating off extra pounds since players held jobs in the offseason and most didn't have the ability to dedicate themselves to staying in shape. Not until Ned Hanlon, manager of the Baltimore Orioles from 1892–98, did a manager use Spring Training to practice baseball skills.

FROM SMALL THINGS Grandstands were added to Al Lang Field in 1947.

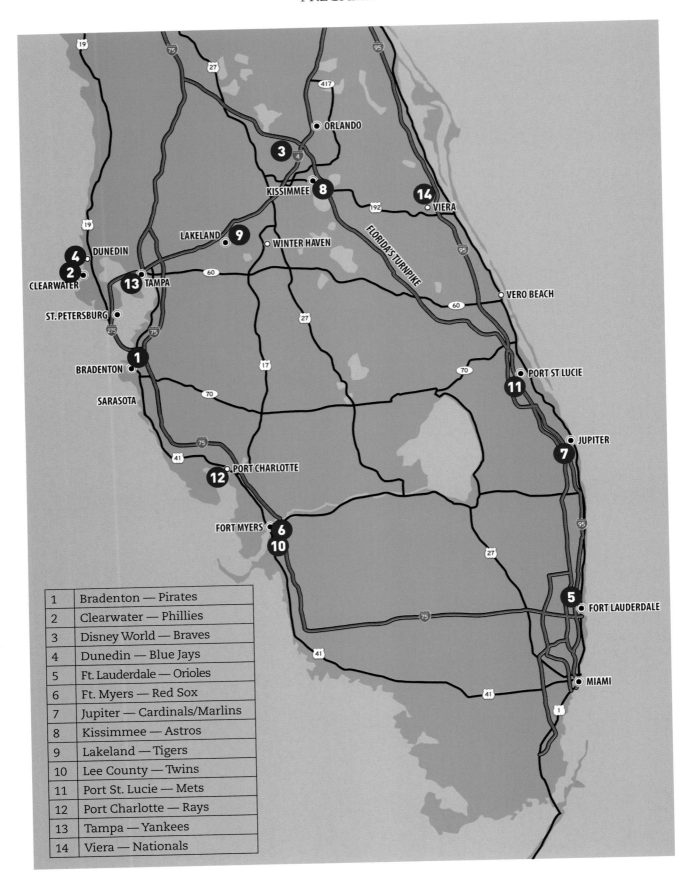

1	Bradenton — Pirates
2	Clearwater — Phillies
3	Disney World — Braves
4	Dunedin — Blue Jays
5	Ft. Lauderdale — Orioles
6	Ft. Myers — Red Sox
7	Jupiter — Cardinals/Marlins
8	Kissimmee — Astros
9	Lakeland — Tigers
10	Lee County — Twins
11	Port St. Lucie — Mets
12	Port Charlotte — Rays
13	Tampa — Yankees
14	Viera — Nationals

GRAPEFRUIT LEAGUE

AFTER MOST TEAMS BEGAN HEADING SOUTH TO TRAIN DURING THE WEEKS BEFORE THE REGULAR season got underway, the next step in the evolution of Spring Training was a slate of exhibition games. The Grapefruit League developed in Florida largely through the tireless efforts of Pittsburgh native Al Lang, who arrived in St. Petersburg, Fla., in 1910. Lang relocated to the Sunshine State at 39 years old, after doctors had told him that respiratory problems left him with just six months to live. A gregarious, lanky, well-dressed man, Lang knew Big Leaguers and baseball executives from his years as a Pittsburgh businessman. In St. Petersburg, his health made a remarkable recovery, which he attributed to the warm weather. As if to repay the community, he spent the rest of his life raising the national profile of his adopted hometown.

Lang lured the Philadelphia Phillies to St. Petersburg for preseason camp in 1915. The Boston Braves arrived in 1922, when the Washington Senators (Tampa), Phillies (Leesburg) and Brooklyn Dodgers (Jacksonville) were the only teams training in Florida. At the time, the rest of baseball was still spread out over California, Georgia, Louisiana and Texas. Thanks to Lang's persistence, the Grapefruit League grew from four teams in 1922 to nine in 1925. Lang had long wanted two teams training in St. Petersburg, and he reached that goal when Yankees Owner Jake Ruppert moved the team to St. Pete from New Orleans in 1924. A decade later, 11 of the 16 Big League clubs trained in Florida. Ruppert had agreed to move the Yankees to Lang's home largely because the city didn't have a reputation for rowdy nightlife and would provide fewer distractions for his marquee player, Babe Ruth. True to his larger-than-life reputation, Ruth still managed to find plenty to do during his off hours in the Tampa Bay area.

Lang "knew Babe Ruth, Lou Gehrig," wrote Wes Singletary, author of *Florida's First Big League Baseball Players*. "He wasn't just some chamber of commerce hustler trying to get teams there. He made sure they knew him."

The Yankees spent 34 years in St. Petersburg, a period that encompassed much of the careers of Ruth, Gehrig, Joe DiMaggio and Mickey Mantle. A new ballpark was built to house the Bronx Bombers in St. Pete after the 1946 season and named for Lang. When the Yankees left for Fort Lauderdale in 1962, the expansion Mets took their place at Al Lang Field, staying through 1987, a year after the club won a World Series title. It seemed the field bestowed magical powers upon its tenants. The New York Giants trained there just one season, 1951, swapping their Phoenix digs with the Yankees. That year the Giants reached the Fall Classic thanks to Bobby Thomson's "Shot Heard 'round the World."

Other Florida cities were also establishing long-term relationships with baseball. In 1934, the Tigers arrived in Lakeland, a modest town of 20,000 best known for citrus farming and a quaint downtown. Lakeland's intermediary with the Tigers was Marcus "Joker" Marchant, the longtime director of the city's parks and recreations department. When the Tigers outgrew their original home at Henley Field, Marchant offered the site of the former Lodwick School of Aeronautics, which had trained thousands of pilots during World War II. With plenty of flat land and barracks, the site soon became "Tiger Town." When a new park was constructed for 1966, it was christened Joker Marchant Stadium.

Although many Florida communities were soon bound to various clubs, perhaps no facility better represented the magic of Spring Training than Dodgertown in Vero Beach, Fla. It opened in 1948 as a self-contained complex so that the Dodgers' African-American players wouldn't have to deal with the era's segregation laws, which would have kept members of the team from lodging or dining together. Dodgertown included six practice fields, its own dorms, a dining hall and, eventually, a golf course. From the start, Dodgertown ranked as the most fan-friendly spring site in baseball, as players walked between fields cordoned off by thin ropes. The Dodgers were the first and only team to own their Spring Training site outright, with Dodgers Owner Walter O'Malley paying $133,087.50 in 1965 for Holman Stadium and the original 60 acres. O'Malley, who lovingly landscaped the property with lush foliage, eventually would expand the site to 465 acres.

CACTUS LEAGUE

Legendary baseball impresario Bill Veeck was the father of too many innovations to name. The Hall of Fame owner grew ivy on the walls of Wrigley Field, placed names on the backs of uniforms, introduced "exploding" scoreboards and perfected the ballpark giveaway. Less known is his role in creating the Cactus League in Arizona. After selling the Brewers in 1945, he retired to a ranch in Arizona, falling in love with the Southwest culture. Not able to stay away from the diamond for long, Veeck purchased the Cleveland Indians in 1946. Shortly thereafter, he moved the team's Spring Training site to Tucson, believing Arizona was more hospitable to African-American players than Florida. Veeck signed Larry Doby, the American League's first black player, in July 1947.

"I had moved our training quarters to Arizona, not so much in preparation for Doby as out of an unpleasant experience with the Milwaukee Brewers," Veeck wrote in his autobiography, *Veeck As In Wreck*.

Veeck then convinced Giants Owner Horace Stoneham to move his team's spring camp to Arizona for four seasons. The Giants and Indians were the only teams in Arizona, with the Giants operating out of Municipal Stadium in Phoenix and the Indians in Tucson's Hi Corbett Field. In 1952, Mesa businessman Dwight Patterson brokered a deal to bring the Cubs, who had been training on California's Catalina Island almost every year since 1922, to Arizona. The growing circuit was officially dubbed "The Cactus League" after the Orioles arrived in Yuma in 1954.

By the 1980s the Cactus League had evolved to include the Cubs, Giants, Indians, Brewers, Angels, A's, Padres and Mariners. In 1994, the city of Peoria, at the time a distant suburb northwest of Phoenix, opened the Peoria Sports Complex for the Padres and Mariners. With a central shared stadium and an equal number of practice fields and training facilities for each team, it became the model for Spring Training sites both in the Southwest and in Florida.

Soon the Grapefruit League was under siege. The White Sox left their longtime home in Sarasota, Fla., to join the expansion Arizona Diamondbacks in Tucson, Ariz., in 1998. In 2000, Florida lawmakers passed a state aid bill that provided funds to help retain Big League franchises. The Florida funding came too late to save the Texas Rangers and Kansas City Royals, though, who left in 2003 to share another two-team complex in Surprise, Ariz., another northwest Phoenix suburb. In 2009, the Indians returned to Arizona to be co-tenants of Goodyear Ballpark, yet another glitzy new dual-team complex, leaving Winter Haven, Fla., without Spring Training for the first time since 1965. After the 2009 season, the Reds joined the Indians in Goodyear, ending a tenure in Florida that dated back to 1923.

Once the Reds arrived in Arizona, Major League Baseball had split its teams evenly for Spring Training, with 15 in Arizona and 15 in Florida. That seems only appropriate for two states that have proven equally hospitable to the national pastime.

1	Glendale — Dodgers/White Sox
2	Goodyear — Indians/Reds
3	Maryvale — Brewers
4	Mesa — Cubs
5	Peoria — Mariners/Padres
6	Phoenix — Athletics
7	Scottsdale — Giants
8	Surprise — Rangers/Royals
9	Tempe — Angels
10	Tucson — Diamondbacks/Rockies

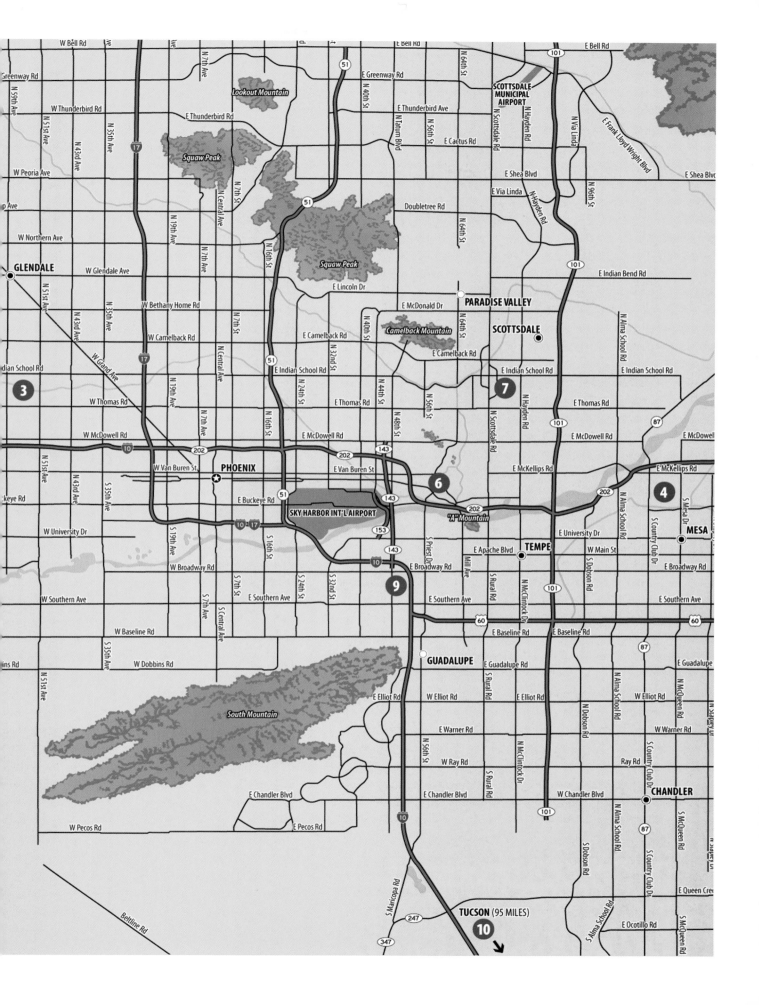

WEEK 1:
A NEW SEASON

SPRING IS A SEASON OF RENEWAL, WHEN THE SPIRIT OF REBIRTH IS PALPABLE IN THE hearts and minds of baseball fans. Even supporters of the previous year's last-place teams can dream of a victory parade. Like managers and general managers, fans envision rookies developing quickly, veterans fighting off Father Time and super-stars staying healthy. By the time pitchers and catchers report to Spring Training in mid-February, clubhouse managers, groundskeepers and traveling secretaries have already been working for weeks.

Fans flock to the opening days of Spring Training in Florida and Arizona, not that there's much to see other than some stretching, pitchers throwing from mounds and infield drills. The clubhouse resembles the first day of school, with a mix of holdovers, young prospects getting their first taste of Big League camp and non-roster journeymen hoping to stretch their careers one more season. During the first week of camp, anything seems possible.

TAKING STOCK Giants clubhouse employees catalog Spring Training supplies in the 1960s.

SOUTHBOUND BABE
Babe Ruth with his wife,
Helen, and daughter, Dorothy,
at Penn Station in New York
as they prepare to leave for
Spring Training in 1923.

ROAD TRIP

TEMPORARILY RELOCATING FOR SPRING TRAINING IS NO EASY TASK FOR A MAJOR LEAGUE team. Although virtually all Spring Training complexes in Arizona and Florida are used by Minor League affiliates during the regular season, Big League clubs bring most of their own equipment.

"Just imagine moving your entire office out of town for six or eight weeks," said Chris Westmoreland, the clubhouse and equipment manager for the Tampa Bay Rays. "You pretty much have to bring everything."

Westmoreland learned that for the first time in 2009 — the first year the Rays did not train in St. Petersburg, mere blocks from where they play during the regular season. In the weeks leading up to Spring Training in 2009, Westmoreland and his staff prepared by staging the move, laying out everything near the loading dock at Tropicana Field to see how many trucks the move would require. After surveying the massive amount of equipment and supplies, he leased a pair of 26-foot trucks for the 90-mile trip south to Port Charlotte.

The Rays clubhouse staff packed the trucks with everything a baseball team might need in the Florida sun, from sunscreen and medical supplies to pine tar and bubble gum. All told, the Rays brought 30 hardcover trunks to Spring Training, as opposed to the 10 or 15 that they might bring on a long regular-season road trip.

Among the items loaded onto the trucks were seven clothing racks packed with uniforms specifically made for Spring Training. Included were the white home jerseys, which would be used for little more than team photo day. There were a whopping 700 dozen (8,400) baseballs; Westmoreland erred on the side of caution when it came to the balls since three of the fields at Charlotte Sports Park — the new site of Rays camp — are bordered by lakes.

Several trunks of video equipment are hauled to camp, as well as boxes packed with letterhead, preseason media guides, research books and printers for the media relations staff. Copies of the regular-season media guide, which becomes available a week or two into Spring Training, are also shipped.

"It's a lot to bring," said Chris Costello, the Rays director of communications. "From a media standpoint, our needs are greater during Spring Training since we have so many more players."

During the preseason, players eat at the ballpark more often, arriving for breakfast and staying through lunch and sometimes a late-afternoon snack or even an early dinner. The Rays packed five huge boxes of plastic bowls, utensils and cups, and three 500-count boxes of 16-ounce soup cups.

Hydration is always important for professional athletes, especially in the heat of Spring Training in Florida and Arizona. The Rays had an entire pallet (25 cases) of Gatorade, with each case containing two dozen 20-ounce bottles. A second pallet contained Gatorade mix and nutrition bars.

The Rays' trucks were packed on the afternoon of Feb. 2 for a departure the following morning. They would arrive later in the day and be unpacked in plenty of time for the arrival of players on Feb. 15. Teams typically take their entire clubhouse staff to Spring Training and everyone is needed, especially in the early weeks when Big League camp can have as many as 70 players.

Just as schoolchildren arrive to a new school year with new clothes and school supplies, players have new equipment. Clubhouse managers from various clubs communicate with one another so they have the right uniform size for new players. Bats are ordered during the offseason and players will retain some from the previous season, especially those that produced hits. Bat manufacturers and shoe companies will ship their wares directly to the Spring Training sites.

In theory, packing for the return trip when camp breaks in late March should be easier, with players having consumed or used many of the supplies. But clubhouse managers often find they need more truck space coming home since players, broadcasters and team personnel are allowed to ship back everything from golf clubs and fishing gear to baby strollers and cribs.

"It's a production," said Westmoreland. "But it's like anything else. The better you pack, the easier things are going to be on the road."

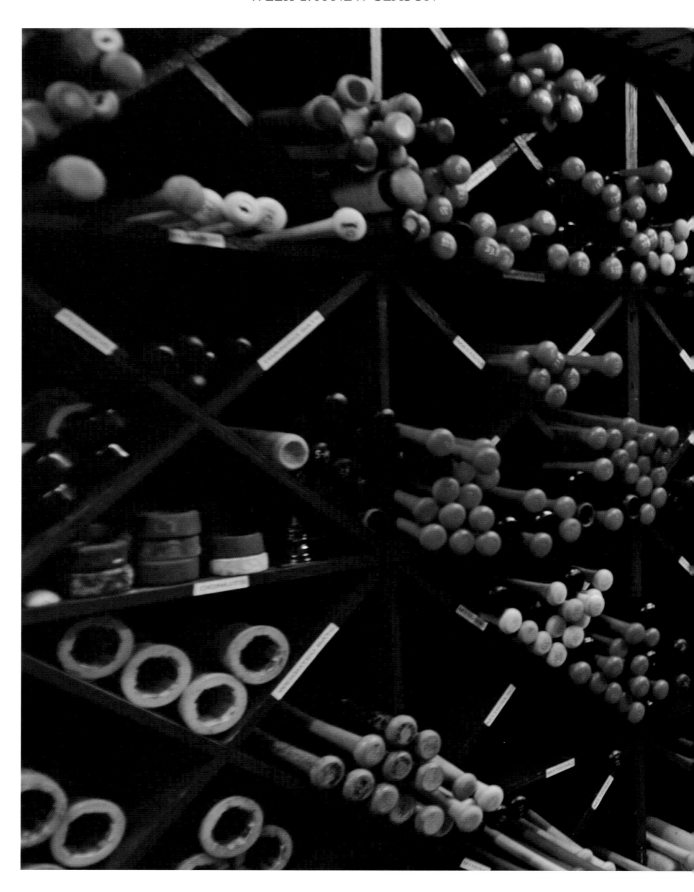

LUMBER YARD Equipment
room at the Giants' Spring
Training facility in Arizona.

PITCHERS AND CATCHERS

THERE'S PERHAPS NO PHRASE MORE EXCITING FOR A BASE-ball fan to hear than "pitchers and catchers report." Many teams, when issuing news releases during the offseason, will even mention how many days until pitchers and catchers report. This group arrives four to six days earlier than position players because it takes longer for pitchers to build up their arm strength to be ready for the season.

"Spring Training is all for the pitchers," said Hall of Fame closer Dennis Eckersley, an analyst for TBS and NESN. "I sure needed it because it took me forever to finally get my velocity back — it took all of Spring Training."

A 60-man Spring Training camp consists of almost half pitchers, five to 10 of whom are non-roster invitees: journeymen longshots hoping to make the team and top young prospects still a few years from making the 40-man roster. Teams start out with about 30 pitchers in camp, which seems like a lot considering that clubs break camp with only 12 or 13. Spring Training gives the managers and coaching staff time to consider options for the Big League staff, as well as monitor the development of prospects who might be called up to the Big Leagues later in the season.

"You can never have too much pitching, even in the spring," said Ed Wade, general manager of the Houston Astros. "You never know what veteran is going to catch a second wind to his career, or what injury might pop up in March."

Catchers, of course, don't need all of this additional preparation for the season, but they're needed early to prepare the pitchers. More catchers are required for Spring Training than could ever be used during the regular season, which is why every Minor League catcher is on hand when camp begins.

During the first days of Spring Training, fans will see basic exercises like the "cover the bag" drill. The pitcher mimes a throw to the plate, a coach chops a grounder to the right of the first baseman and the pitcher beats the imaginary runner to the bag and takes a throw. After the winter months, fans gladly watch such routine drills.

Having pitchers and catchers arrive early also allows clubhouse staff to gradually build up to full capacity. Unlike the cramped facilities of past spring ballparks, today's clubhouses are designed to house 50 or 60 players. Still, it's easier to get 30 or 35 batterymates situated first and deal with the position players four or five days later.

FIRING LINE Gerald Laird (second from right) of the Detroit Tigers works out with fellow catchers early in 2009 Spring Training in Lakeland, Fla.

REPORTING FOR DUTY
Red Sox pitchers arrive for
workouts on Feb. 20, 2005, at
Boston's Spring Training facility
in Fort Myers, Fla.

CHORUS LINE Cardinals players warm up before a 2005 workout at Roger Dean Stadium in Jupiter, Fla.

FIRST PITCH Giants pitcher Ed Halicki throws with teammates in camp at Casa Grande, Ariz., in the 1970s.

BACK TO SCHOOL

THE FIRST WEEK OF SPRING TRAINING IS NOT UNLIKE THE first week of high school. With players shuffled over the winter through trades, free agency, retirements and the development of young talent, the clubhouse is a mix of new players and holdovers from the previous season. Newcomers to the organization often arrive with the duffel bags provided by their former teams, which are unloaded and hoisted atop lockers, temporarily giving the clubhouse the feel of an All-Star Game. Clubhouse managers eventually remove the bags from other clubs and issue new ones.

New players will often make rounds of the clubhouse shaking hands, although introductions are not always necessary. These days, ballplayers from different teams often get to know one another through various offseason conditioning camps, winter leagues or even while playing together in the World Baseball Classic. Much like a ninth grader finds himself reunited with some of his classmates from previous years, most veterans discover at least a handful of familiar faces upon arriving at camp in February.

"It is a lot like the first day of school," said well-traveled outfielder Gabe Kapler. "That's the perfect analogy. It's all about first impressions and trying to remember all of the names, which is daunting when you come to a new place. There's always that embarrassing moment where you say, 'Nice to meet you' and you're reminded that you've met several times previously."

Kapler found plenty of former teammates upon arriving in the Rays' spring clubhouse for the first time in 2009. He had played with first baseman Carlos Pena in Boston, reliever Brian Shouse in Colorado and outfielder Gabe Gross with the Brewers. He did not, thankfully, meet anyone he had managed during a stint at Class-A Greenville (S.C.) in 2007 before making a comeback as a player. "That might have been a little strange," he admitted.

In 1996, Tony La Russa's first year managing the Cardinals, his camp in St. Petersburg, Fla., included a dozen players and coaches who had played under him in Oakland, including Dennis Eckersley, Todd Stottlemyre and Willie McGee. The team's general manager at the time, Walt Jocketty, was another Oakland alum who helped make La Russa feel at home. Unfortunately, not every player walks into camp already having several friends on the club. Those players have to meet new teammates and establish relationships from scratch.

"Normally I like to get to camp early so I can get to know all the new faces. I don't think that will take too long here," said Mike Gallego about his teammates with the Cardinals in 1996.

For younger, lesser-known players, especially those not likely to make the Big League club, the first few days with a new organization can be intimidating.

"You need to learn the organization, the people in it, how it operates, the mentality and dynamic of it," said Dirk Hayhurst, a relief pitcher who made his way to the Blue Jays camp in 2009 after being waived by the Padres.

"Is it an open environment? How do you interact? Those are the dynamics that make a team a team. For me, my confidence is derived in some part from the people I'm around. Can I go to this coach when I'm struggling? Is he going to be sympathetic or hard on me? Will they expect me to know everything or will they be willing to teach me to make me better?"

Players quickly find that each clubhouse has its own personality based largely on the veterans already there.

"Some clubhouses are quiet. Some a little uptight, some are loose, some are really funny and some are not so funny," said 17-year veteran Cliff Floyd. "You have to find your niche and see who you can talk to, who is really serious, who doesn't like to joke or talk much. You check in where you fit in."

Outfielder Coco Crisp, who joined the Kansas City Royals in 2009, wasn't worried about moving to his third team in five seasons. After all, he attended four different high schools and two colleges. "You blend in right away," Crisp said. "You do have to learn the structure of camp, which can be slightly different. Plus every team has some slightly different philosophies. Other than that, it's pretty smooth."

For veteran players starting with a new team in the spring, it can be an easier transition than for younger guys, especially for those vets returning to their original organization. Tom Glavine returned to the Braves' complex at Disney's Wide World of Sports in 2008 after five seasons with the Mets and assumed his old locker near longtime friends John Smoltz and Chipper Jones.

In 2009, Jason Giambi returned to Phoenix Municipal Stadium and the Oakland A's after seven seasons with the Yankees. Although the players in the clubhouse were different and the ballpark had been remodeled, Giambi quickly reestablished his role as clubhouse leader.

"I guess the biggest change is seeing guys you knew as players now on the coaching staff," Giambi said. "But even with so much time passing, it's like coming home."

> These days, ballplayers from different teams often get to know one another through various offseason conditioning camps, winter leagues or even while playing together in the World Baseball Classic.

LEATHER EXPO
Curtis Granderson of the Tigers looks over a couple of gloves during 2009 Spring Training at Joker Marchant Stadium in Lakeland, Fla.

BAG MEN Equipment bags lay on the field before daily workouts during 2009 Spring Training at Detroit Tigers camp in Lakeland, Fla.

PREGAME FACE
A's players bond while
eating lunch before a
Spring Training game
at Phoenix Municipal
Stadium in 2005.

TRAVEL PLANS

DURING THE REGULAR SEASON, A TEAM'S TRAVELING SECRETARY is responsible for chartering airplanes, booking hotel rooms and arranging ground transportation for a traveling party of roughly 55 to 60 people, a number that includes players, coaches, trainers, broadcasters and support staff. Today's road-weary players and coaches expect stress-free, first-class travel.

Thankfully, Spring Training travel presents far fewer challenges, if only because most spring travel consists only of day trips by bus. Teams reserve large blocks of rooms at hotels near the training camps, but they generally are used only by staff and Minor Leaguers; the Big Leaguers tend to rent private condos. Players on the 40-man roster receive first-class airline tickets to Spring Training. Non-roster players receive coach-class airline tickets or mileage reimbursement if they drive.

Grapefruit League teams must endure longer bus rides than their Cactus League counterparts since spring camps are more spread out in Florida than in Arizona. Trips for Grapefruit clubs can last up to three hours and require 7:30 a.m. departures. Managers make it a point not to load any one player up with too many of the longer trips.

It's not unusual for a team to make an overnight trip during Spring Training. The Philadelphia Phillies or Detroit Tigers, for instance, might travel to Jupiter's Roger Dean Stadium to face the St. Louis Cardinals one day and the Florida Marlins the next.

With 12 teams now training in the greater Phoenix region, it's rare that a team has to stay overnight in Tucson, although the Tucson-based Arizona Diamondbacks and Colorado Rockies often will play back-to-back games in the Phoenix area, requiring an overnight stay. This is not a hard sell to players — especially the Diamondbacks, many of whom have homes in Phoenix for the regular season.

"I still run a bus back and forth, and sometimes there aren't many guys on it," said Roger Riley, the director of team travel for the D-backs, who finds most of the players take their own cars.

A traveling secretary's job gets a little hectic as Spring Training progresses and cuts are made. Those assigned to the Minor Leagues need only relocate to another part of camp. Those released outright receive a plane ticket back home or, hopefully for them, reimbursement for travel to another team's Spring Training facility.

GROUNDSKEEPERS

NOBODY WORKS HARDER DURING SPRING TRAINING THAN members of grounds crews. With many spring complexes consisting of as many as seven fields — 14 if two clubs share a facility — there's no shortage of grass, dirt and equipment that needs tending, making 15-hour days routine

Hall of Famer George Brett recalls arriving at the Royals former complex in Baseball City, Fla., at 6:30 a.m. during Spring Training and finding legendary groundskeeper George Toma already hard at work. Toma's spring schedule is not unusual. Even before players arrive, the grounds crew is watering, manicuring and otherwise preparing the fields for a busy day of activity. Unlike the concrete stadiums built at the Spring Training sites of years past, today's facilities usually are surrounded by grass and lush foliage, which also need to be maintained.

Most spring parks built in the last 15 years also feature a berm beyond the outfield wall. The sloped grassy area provides fans a good vantage point to watch the game from beach towels. But it can be a high-maintenance area given the traffic it endures in March.

Florida residents typically grow St. Augustine grass, a durable crabgrass hybrid that's resistant to drought and insects. Since it grows like vines, it's too thick and spongy for athletic use, so most Grapefruit League ballparks use a blend of Bermuda and rye grasses. In Arizona, Spring Training ballparks tend to feature blends of Bermuda, rye and Kentucky blue grass, not unlike the turf used for golf courses.

While the grass gets most of the attention from spectators, players are concerned with the clay. After all, that's what determines infield bounces, the feel of the pitcher's mound and how well a batter can dig into the box.

"Everybody thinks a groundskeeper spends all his time on the grass, but in baseball the grass is secondary," said the 80-year-old Toma, who still serves as a turf consultant for the Twins and the NFL. "The infield, pitching mound and home plate come first."

In the early-morning hours, sprinklers water the grass throughout a Spring Training complex. On game days, the grounds crew begins preparing for batting practice around 8:30 a.m., going

SUN SHOWER
The Nationals' grounds crew readies the field at Space Coast Stadium.

through a routine similar to the early-afternoon regular-season schedule. They begin by placing a batting cage at home plate. A triangular tarp goes over the first few feet of the diamond extending from the batter's box to protect the grass from heavy traffic during batting practice.

An L-shaped screen is placed in front of the pitcher's mound to shield the batting-practice pitcher and can be positioned on either side depending on whether the pitcher throws from the right or left. There are screens at first, second and third base to protect players going through infield drills and one placed up the middle, at the edge of the outfield, to protect whoever is gathering balls returned from the outfield.

With a 1:05 p.m. start, a grounds crew member often can get home for dinner time, although the 7 p.m. contests late in the spring make for some long days.

Similar to the regular season, the grounds crew is on-call throughout each Spring Training exhibition contest. The crew drags the infield during the game and is ready for rain delays and any in-game alterations needed to the field. Once the game is over, there's mowing to be done — fields typically are mowed daily — along with mound repair and periodic edging along the infield.

A DAY IN THE LIFE OF A GROUNDS CREW

Mike Williams is the Head Groundskeeper for the Charleston RiverDogs, a Class-A Yankees affiliate in South Carolina. He was Head Groundskeeper for the New York Mets from 2001–03 and the Tampa Bay Rays from 1997–2000. Here is a typical Spring Training day for Williams during his time as a Big League groundskeeper:

6–8:30 a.m.: Arrive at the field. Meet with coaches and manager about specific field requests. Finish the mulling and clay work; get the proper moisture on the infield; put the bases in; and dew drag.

8:30 a.m.: Check each field at the Spring Training facility, and make sure all are ready to be used by both Major League and Minor League teams by 9 a.m.

9–1 p.m.: Players begin working out at 9 a.m. Grounds crew continues to deal with specific training and equipment requests. Coordination with coaches and baseball operations is key when adjusting to changing weather.

1–4 p.m.: Major League games and Minor League scrimmages take place on most days. Grounds crew finds 30 to 40 minutes to eat lunch after contests are underway. The grounds staff is like the 10th man in the lineup, though, and must be available when needed.

4–4:30 p.m.: There is usually a batting practice, for anywhere from 30 to 90 minutes after games. Pitching machines are set up for BP. If it rains, set up inside.

6 p.m.: Start to prepare for the following day of practice and games when BP finishes. Preparation includes everything from dealing with specific problems that arose that day to making sure all fields are properly mowed.

7 p.m.: Depart facility.

RAIN MEN Members of the Chicago Cubs grounds crew squeegee water from the tarp onto the grass to get ready for a Spring Training game between the Cubs and the Giants in 2004.

WEEK 2: SHAPING UP

The second week of Spring Training is perhaps the most exciting one for fans, managers and club personnel. With position players arriving, the squad takes shape. The possibilities seem endless with as many as 65 players in camp, giving a manager numerous options — and decisions — at every position.

Exhibition games begin during the second week of camp, allowing fans to get their first glimpses of the countless lineup permutations that spring brings. Initially, just a handful of veterans play in the exhibitions, and those first-string players usually last just a few innings before heading for the showers. Starting pitchers usually toss no more than 30 pitches per outing at this stage. Young prospects and non-roster players see the bulk of the action, so during this time fans get their best look at tomorrow's stars.

For what the exhibitions lack in midseason drama, they more than make up for in atmosphere. With most of North America still shivering, fans in Arizona and Florida lather up with sunscreen and get a jumpstart on the new season.

RUN IN THE SUN Players working out on the warning track during a game at Tigers camp in 1987.

WELCOME TO TOWN

WHILE PITCHERS NEED THE FULL SIX WEEKS OF SPRING TRAINING TO build their arm strength and pitch counts, today's position players don't need nearly as long to get ready for Opening Day. Decades ago, position players used Spring Training as a conditioning camp, sweating off the winter pounds while getting into "baseball shape." By the time a position player reports to camp these days, usually four to six days after the pitchers and catchers arrive, he's actually in the best shape of the year.

Unlike previous generations of ballplayers, today's Big Leaguers spend the six weeks before Spring Training participating in strenuous offseason conditioning programs. During the last decade, training facilities such as the Athletes' Performance Institute have sprung up to cater to professional athletes preparing for upcoming seasons.

API, which has facilities in Arizona, Florida and California, has trained numerous Big Leaguers, including Carl Crawford, Nomar Garciaparra, Pat Burrell, Dustin Pedroia, Kevin Youkilis, Brian Roberts, Manny Ramirez, Justin Morneau and Vernon Wells. Programs such as API stress strength training and conditioning that emphasizes the "core region" of the shoulders, torso and hips — the key areas for all baseball movement.

"This is our pre–Spring Training training," Youkilis said. "The idea is to get into the best shape of the year, so from day one of Spring Training you can focus on baseball-specific work, which you really can't simulate until you get to camp."

Pirates second baseman Freddy Sanchez trained at API prior to his All-Star seasons of 2006 and '07. "It makes a huge difference," he said. "The season is a marathon and everyone comes into Spring Training in such good shape. I don't know how guys did it back in the day. If I didn't do anything in the offseason, I'd be dragging by July."

Adam Jones, the Orioles young center fielder, sought the attention of API trainers in Arizona during the winter of 2009. The extra work Jones did during the offseason paid dividends as soon as the 2009 season began. By June, Jones had already slugged 11 home runs, two more than his total for the entire 2008 season, and he was hitting at better than a .340 clip. Jones, along with others who endure grueling offseason workouts, hope that superior conditioning can mean the difference between being a solid ballplayer and being an All-Star.

Countless other Major League stars joined Jones in Tempe, Ariz., in the early part of 2009. Also present were Pedroia — fresh off his 2008 American League MVP Award — Youkilis, Crawford, Roberts and Curt Schilling, who eventually decided to retire prior to the start of the season.

Although team strength coaches prefer players to work in-house, teams increasingly recognize the role of the outside training facilities. The Red Sox and Dodgers have established a consulting arrangement with API. The New York Yankees, on the other hand, manage to attract a number of players, including Derek Jeter, to train at their Minor League complex in

CASUAL CALISTHENICS
Kevin Youkilis (right) and Brian Roberts train at the Athletes' Performance Institute in Tempe, Ariz., in January 2005.

LEAN INTO IT
Prospect and 1999
first-round draft pick
Ricky Asadoorian
performs a lunge with
a twist while Mark
Verstegen monitors hi
form during a work-
out at API in Tempe
in January 2005.

Tampa, just down the road from George M. Steinbrenner Field, the Yankees' Spring Training home. But that's mostly because so many players live in Tampa during the offseason. Convenience is, of course, a major factor, especially when players are faced with shrinking an already short offseason.

All things considered, it's tough for strength coaches to complain when position players arrive to camp in terrific shape, even if they are a little tardy. Tony La Russa, during his years as manager of the Oakland Athletics, didn't object too strenuously to the predictable late arrival of Rickey Henderson, one of the best conditioned players in baseball history.

Conversely, La Russa couldn't help but be impressed in 1996, his first spring as manager of the Cardinals, when veteran Ray Lankford reported several days early to camp in St. Petersburg, Fla. The outfielder's hard work paid off later that season as he was selected to participate in the All-Star Game.

"I've never had an outfielder show up this early," La Russa told Lankford at the time. "You just let me know what Spring Training games you want to take off."

Unlike Lankford, many position players believe Spring Training is too long, a theory that was put to the test in 1995, when the eight-month players' strike ended and players had just three weeks of Spring Training.

"We all had to hurry up to get ready," recalled Hall of Famer Cal Ripken. "There was some anxiety about getting ready in time, but I thought that was the perfect amount of time for a regular player to get ready. To get that many at-bats and to start to play, you can begin to play in the seventh and eighth and ninth inning pretty easily. When you start seeing pitches it all seems to come back."

NO REST FOR THE WEARY

The Athletes' Performance Institute (API) believes that "in the game of life, there is no offseason."

Some of baseball's elite athletes, including several All-Stars and World Series champions, have come through the doors of API in Arizona, California and Florida with similar mindsets. These players seek the expertise of API President Mark Verstegen and his team of trainers during the winter months to prepare both mentally and physically for the upcoming season.

With the goal of bolstering an athlete's overall career achievements, decreasing injury potential and offering strategies for future success, API designs workout programs unique to each player. "Baseball Performance Speed Week" is dedicated solely to maximizing agility for runners on the basepaths and fielders on the diamond, while "Baseball Performance Training for Pitchers" is geared toward fine-tuning the talents of those who call the mound home. The API at the Andrews Institute in Gulf Breeze, Fla., is especially focused on rehabilitative training.

Rather than focus exclusively on weight lifting, those who utilize the facilities find themselves employing targeted core and strength training workouts, combined with new dietary regimens, to produce results. Sessions at API serve as a precursor to the rigors of Spring Training for baseball greats and other professional competitors; programs are also available at API for high school– and college-level athletes.

MAKING STRIDES Big Leaguers Jerry Hairston (left) and Lou Merloni train at API in Tempe, Ariz., in 2005.

DIME A DOZEN
Players perform
calisthenics at Dodgers
camp during Spring
Training in 1948.

BATTLE OF THE STATES

ASKING AN AVID BASEBALL FAN TO CHOOSE BETWEEN SPRING Training in Florida or Arizona is like asking a cocoa lover to pick between chocolate mousse and chocolate cake; after all, there is no downside to either.

Florida, with its beaches, theme parks and long history as both a Spring Training site and spring break destination for college students, has always been popular with fans and players. Arizona, with its golf courses, desert beauty and attractions such as the city of Sedona and the Grand Canyon, is equally inviting.

For many years, Florida held an edge in the minds of many baseball organizations. As recently as 1997, the Sunshine State hosted 20 teams for Spring Training, while Arizona had just eight. Of those eight clubs, the Colorado Rockies played in Tucson, two hours from Phoenix — the hub of Spring Training in the Southwest.

In the last 12 years, though, Arizona has added six teams, five that previously spent the spring in Florida and the expansion Arizona Diamondbacks. The 15 teams in the revamped Cactus League are also closer together now thanks to the completion of the 101 freeway at the turn of the century.

To reach the Peoria Sports Complex, the palatial home to the San Diego Padres and Seattle Mariners, fans traveling from Phoenix and Scottsdale used to have to navigate the endless commercial sprawl and stoplights of Bell Road. Once an oasis in the midst of a vast desert, the Peoria Sports Complex is just a hundred yards from the freeway now, surrounded by hotels and bustling chain restaurants such as The Cheesecake Factory and P.F. Chang's. A trip from Scottsdale that took well over an hour in 1999 takes half as long today.

By hosting two clubs with equal facilities, Peoria became the model for new Spring Training complexes in Surprise, Goodyear and Glendale, each featuring a central stadium surrounded on each side by a clubhouse and six fields for each of the two Big League tenants. Each of the three new sites in Arizona, housing six teams collectively, is located just off the freeway.

Fans in Phoenix can watch two teams work out in the morning and make it to another complex by 1 p.m. for a game. If there's a 7 p.m. contest, as there often is late in the spring, they can make it there with time to spare, assuming the game is not in Tucson.

"It makes things so convenient," said San Diego Padres General Manager Kevin Towers. "I can watch a Minor League game at our complex at 10 a.m. and still make it to the Big League game anywhere in the valley. You just can't do that in Florida."

In Florida, teams are much more spread out, especially with the recent departures of five teams to Arizona and the Tampa Bay

ARIZONA

Cactus League
Established: 1947
Teams: 15 (8 NL and 7 AL)
 Angels, Athletics, Brewers, Cubs, Diamondbacks, Dodgers, Giants, Indians, Mariners, Padres, Rangers, Rockies, Royals, White Sox
Ballparks: 11
 Tempe Diablo Stadium (Angels)
 Phoenix Municipal Stadium (Athletics)
 Maryvale Stadium (Brewers)
 Hohokam Park (Cubs)
 Tucson Electric Park (Diamondbacks)
 Camelback Ranch (Dodgers, White Sox)
 Scottsdale Stadium (Giants)
 Goodyear Ballpark (Indians, Reds)
 Peoria Sports Complex (Mariners, Padres)
 Surprise Stadium (Rangers, Royals)
 Hi Corbett Field (Rockies)
Population: 6.5 million
Nickname: Grand Canyon State
Average Temperature in March: 76°F

Rays moving from St. Petersburg to Port Charlotte. Fans in the Tampa Bay area still have three teams within a half-hour drive — the Phillies, Blue Jays and Yankees — although for many years the area also hosted the Cardinals, Reds, Rays and Orioles.

The Cardinals and Marlins, who share a complex in Jupiter, Fla., face each other six times during the spring and have short trips to Port St. Lucie to face the Mets and Fort Lauderdale to play the Orioles. For any other game, though, they face a minimum two-hour drive.

"You have some early-morning bus rides in Florida," said Jason Giambi, who as a member of the Oakland A's and the Yankees has seen both extremes of Spring Training travel. "You get around so much quicker in Arizona."

Joe Torre spent the bulk of his long career as a player and manager training in Florida, including at storied sites such as Al Lang Field and Dodgertown. But he recognizes the practical advantages of the Dodgers' new home in Arizona.

"Teams are more concentrated," he said. "That makes sense because if you want to get work done in Spring Training, the less time you're on the road, the better. That's the biggest issue of Spring Training — not who you play, but how much work you can get done."

ANGELS AND DIABLOS
The Angels have called
Tempe Diablo Stadium in
Arizona home since 1993.

BANNER DAY The Giants moved from New York to San Francisco in 1958, but they had already trained in Phoenix for six years.

BASEBALL ON THE BAY Al Lang Field in St. Petersburg, Fla.,
has been the Spring Training home to the Cardinals, Mets and Rays.

Because of the proximity of camps in Arizona, clubs are more likely to take batting practice at home and then take a late-morning bus ride to the away game. In Florida, teams typically board a bus at 8 a.m. and work out at the opponent's complex before the game.

Jay Buckley, owner of Wisconsin-based Jay Buckley's Baseball Tours, finds it most advantageous to base his Florida spring tour in Orlando. Although there are only three trips within an hour (Braves, Astros, Tigers), it's possible to reach virtually every Grapefruit League camp within a two-and-a-half-hour drive.

"It's definitely more of a challenge to hit every camp in Florida," Buckley said. "But for a lot of fans, just driving around is part of the spring experience."

First baseman Casey Kotchman sees the benefits of both locales. He began his career with the Angels, traveling short distances from Tempe, Ariz., during Spring Training. Playing for the Braves, whose spring home is in Kissimmee, Fla., he endures longer bus trips. At the same time, he grew up in the Tampa Bay area, not far from the spring homes of the Yankees, Phillies and Blue Jays, along with the Rays, Orioles and Cardinals, who trained there during his childhood.

"I love Arizona and Florida, but I guess I'm biased because I grew up where I did," he said. "You can go to the beach and fish in Florida, and play just as much golf as you can in Arizona. That's pretty appealing whether you're a fan or a player."

FLORIDA

Grapefruit League
Established: 1913
Teams: 15 (8 NL and 7 AL)
  Astros, Blue Jays, Braves, Cardinals, Marlins, Mets, Nationals, Orioles, Phillies, Pirates, Rays, Reds, Red Sox, Tigers, Twins, Yankees
Ballparks: 15
  Osceola Stadium (Astros)
  Dunedin Stadium (Blue Jays)
  Champion Stadium (Braves)
  Roger Dean Stadium (Cardinals, Marlins)
  Tradition Field (Mets)
  Space Coast Stadium (Nationals)
  Ft. Lauderdale Stadium (Orioles)
  Bright House Networks Field (Phillies)
  McKechnie Field (Pirates)
  Charlotte Sports Park (Rays)
  City of Palms Park (Red Sox)
  Joker Marchant Stadium (Tigers)
  Hammond Stadium (Twins)
  George M. Steinbrenner Field (Yankees)
Population: 18.3 million
Nickname: Sunshine State
Average Temperature in March: 79°F

Torre has spent the bulk of his career as a player and manager training in Florida, including at such storied sites as Dodgertown. But he recognizes the practical advantages of the Dodgers' new home in Arizona.

BASEBALL HEAVEN The Dodgers trained in their legendary Vero Beach location from 1948–2008.

PHOTO DAY

TEAMS RARELY WEAR THEIR REGULAR-SEASON UNIFORMS DURING SPRING TRAINING, OPTING instead for batting practice jerseys during exhibition games. With clubs eschewing home and road jerseys, it's not uncommon for both teams to wear the same color jersey, like when the Blue Jays and Yankees each wear blue. The unusual uniform choices give exhibition contests a look distinct from the regular season.

But this presents a problem for photographers, who prefer to shoot pictures of players wearing their "home whites," especially those players new to the organization. Both the clubs and outside organizations generally want photos that don't look like they were shot during the spring and can be used all season long, whether they're for magazines, trading cards or online use. When a franchise undergoes a radical uniform redesign, as the Padres did prior to 2004, the team will assist photographers by wearing the home whites several times during spring exhibitions.

Otherwise, photographers must rely on "Photo Day" for the shots they need of players in their regular-season garb. MLB Photos coordinates with public relations officials — one located in Arizona and another in Florida — to schedule Photo Day for each club. Teams are allotted a morning in late February and typically set up an indoor studio for portraits and an area on the field for action shots. There are usually about 15 to 20 different photographers at each camp. Players shuttle between stations in small groups, relaxing in the clubhouse until called upon.

Wire services such as The Associated Press and Getty Images send photographers. So do trading card manufacturers and other producers of officially licensed MLB products. Photographers who cover more than one team map out their Photo Day tours of Spring Training camps carefully. Although MLB Photos works with PR officials in each Spring Training state and with each club to create a schedule that avoid conflicts, some teams inevitably have to stage it on the same days. In these instances, the editors at the various organizations must prioritize and assign photographers accordingly.

Overall, MLB Photos will take more than 11,000 shots combined. At each club's Photo Day, MLB Photos also works in conjunction with Fox, who creates digital "cut-out" images of each player for use on scoreboards and in television broadcasts. It's also a busy day for official team photographers, who shoot players for media guides and the assorted team publications that will be made available during the season.

"We even shoot ID photos for club personnel," said Jay Stenhouse, the Blue Jays vice president of communications. "It's about the only time when you have a captive audience."

Since Photo Day is generally held so early on in Spring Training, every player invited to Big League camp is available for the event, including top prospects and non-roster invitees who may not be with the club come Opening Day. Prospects will be photographed in their Big League uniforms for the first time on Photo Day. Those photos inevitably find their way into trading card sets and are often featured on the player's rookie card, which is coveted by collectors. These images also come in handy once the player is promoted to the Majors. When that occurs, the team doesn't have to scramble for an updated image for the scoreboard video screen or media guide supplement.

All non-roster players are also shot since one or two usually end up on the Opening Day squad. The rest of the photos go unused, in some cases becoming interesting conversation pieces for noteworthy players who never made the team. After all, who remembers that Roberto Alomar donned a Tampa Bay Devil Rays uniform during Spring Training of 2005 before announcing his retirement? Or that Jose Canseco played for the Anaheim Angels and Montreal Expos during Spring Training late in his career, getting released both times?

Such information does not appear on baseball cards. Any visual evidence, if it exists, likely comes from Photo Day.

STRIKE A POSE
The Athletics' Scott Hatteberg smiles for the camera during Photo Day in 2005.

STANDING ROOM ONLY The D-backs participate in a Spring Training game at Tucson Electric Park in 1998.

FIRST GAMES

EVEN DIE-HARD BASEBALL FANS MAY BE A LITTLE TAKEN ABACK THE first time they watch a Spring Training game. Lineups bear only vague resemblances to the regular season, especially during the first week of competition, when veterans play no more than a few innings. Some contests at the start of the spring do not even feature two Big League teams, with college teams from either the local area or the Major League club's home market invited to play. In recent years, the Braves have played the University of Georgia, the Cardinals faced St. Louis University and the Red Sox have squared off against Boston College during Spring Training. Likewise, the Marlins have tangled with the University of Miami and the Tigers played Florida Southern College, located a few miles from Joker Marchant Stadium in Lakeland, Fla.

Teams generally field at least four regulars in each exhibition game to give paying fans a representative sampling of the actual roster. This unofficial rule presents more of a challenge in Florida, where veterans cringe at the prospect of long bus trips each day. Managers attempt to keep veteran players from enduring too many long rides.

In some cases, though, players may actually ask to make certain trips. The Diamondbacks have no trouble getting players to make the two-hour trip from Tucson to a game in greater Phoenix, especially if the player can spend the night in his own bed and play another game in the area the following day. The same is true for Rays Manager Joe Maddon, now that his club trains in Port Charlotte — two hours away from its regular-season home in St. Pete.

For several years, fans of the Rays and Yankees got to see full regular-season lineups whenever the teams faced off, even during the first week of Spring Training. In the late 1990s, when Tampa Bay was struggling and the Yankees were in the midst of winning four World Series in five years, there was little rivalry between the teams. But Owners George Steinbrenner and Vince Naimoli, both Tampa residents, were fierce competitors and then-managers Joe Torre and Larry Rothschild knew that their respective bosses wanted them to treat such spring exhibitions like midseason clashes.

"It was always clear to us that we couldn't lose to three teams," former Yankees reliever Jeff Nelson once said, "the Red Sox, Mets and Devil Rays."

Most Spring Training games are not so intense. Some managers sit on chairs outside the dugout. In some parks, sportswriters linger in the dugout and interview players up until gametime, sometimes standing alongside them for the National Anthem. Relief pitchers occasionally will sign autographs from the bullpen during the game. Players who have exited the game or have the day off will run wind sprints along the outfield warning track, dodging fly balls if necessary. It's all part of the laid-back atmosphere of Spring Training, which most veterans treat as a leisurely warm-up to the regular season.

"You don't want to peak too early down here," said Padres outfielder Brian Giles. "The goal is that when you break camp here, you feel 100 percent. The games mean nothing. It's all about how you feel."

FATHER-SON GAME
Pitcher David Riske with his
son, Payton, before a Spring
Training contest in 2005.

GOT 'EM A young fan peeks at a spring game, hoping for an autograph.

CALMING EFFECT
Fiery Lou Piniella shows
his relaxed side while
talking to reporters during
Spring Training.

MEDIA COVERAGE

FOR A BASEBALL WRITER, SPRING TRAINING CAN BE THE BEST part of the season. Writers welcome the opportunity to head to Florida or Arizona, escaping the February cold of their home cities. Their newspapers usually rent furnished condos for six to eight weeks, accommodations sometimes located near beaches and golf courses.

Although it can sound like a vacation, the spring does not provide many opportunities for relaxation. Unlike the regular season, when beat writers arrive at the ballpark around 3 p.m., it's usually necessary to show up at the Spring Training complex before 8 a.m. Upon arriving, writers make a quick stop in the press box to leave their laptops and head straight to the clubhouse, where players are available until taking the field for stretching, generally around 9:30.

Most managers then speak with beat writers while players are working out. The conversation tends to focus on injury updates, roster moves, lineup decisions and the previous game. This session lasts about 15 minutes. If the team is playing at home, writers will head back to the press box to file reports for their newspaper's blog and work on feature stories until the team heads back to the clubhouse, usually around 11:15. If the team is playing on the road, the writers might opt to get a head start on the drive to the opponent's facility.

In Arizona, where camps are bunched together, reporters usually don't have to worry about fitting in a long drive as part of their pre-game routine. In Florida, though, drives can be as long as three hours, and coverage can present a challenge. If a newspaper has two reporters with the team, one drives ahead to the away game and the other stays back with the players left behind at camp — often the team's biggest stars, who have more time for interviews since they're not playing.

In addition to beat writers, there also are many "national" baseball reporters. They don't cover one specific team, but report for newspapers, magazines, online outlets or television. They float around Arizona and Florida, reporting on specific stories and trends. Like the beat writers, they arrive early, but they have the luxury of leaving before or during the game because the exhibition games themselves are not especially newsworthy on a national level. The beat writers stay until the last out, of course, as it's their job to chronicle all developments for the fans from a team's hometown. Their daily coverage tends to focus on how pitchers are progressing, who is making a strong bid to make the team and who is or is not recovering from injuries.

Until recent years, beat writers typically would file *just* two stories a day: a feature-oriented story on one player or team development, such as the club placing a greater emphasis on speed or defense; and a "notebook," mentioning transactions, injuries and interesting tidbits from the clubhouse.

These days, with news available instantly online, writers blog all day long, providing up-to-the-moment news and analysis for fans back home. As is the case during the regular season, they write during the game, keeping one eye — or at least one ear — on the action from the press box. Unlike the regular season, pitchers are available for interviews upon leaving the game, with the clubhouse seemingly filled only with Minor Leaguers by game's end.

Because of the laid-back nature of Spring Training, there are few restrictions to media coverage. Members of the press must still wear credentials; most receive an "all parks" pass that allows them access to all facilities in Florida and Arizona.

Writers typically leave the ballpark around dinner time, although some in Florida face a significant drive back home, a trip that can begin in the midst of rush hour. Dinner often is the highlight of the day, with writers flocking to such popular restaurants as Don & Charlie's Steakhouse in Scottsdale, Ariz., and Frenchy's on Clearwater Beach in Florida.

For the most part, though, the long, leisurely spring dinners that writers tended to enjoy are a thing of the past. Many writers use the early evenings to squeeze in a workout, catch a quick glimpse of the sunset, and prepare for another day of feeding the insatiable 24/7 news cycle.

A SPRING TRAINING DAY IN THE LIFE OF A BEAT REPORTER

Richard Justice covers the Astros for the *Houston Chronicle* and has been a regular at the club's Spring Training site in Kissimmee, Fla., over the years.

8–9 a.m.: Arrive at Osceola Stadium when clubhouse opens. Meet with players before pregame warmups.

9 a.m.–12 p.m.: Wander the fields; chat with players, club officials, trainers, scouts and fans. When squad travels for away game, visit with those players staying behind, then hit the road to meet the team.

12–12:30 p.m.: Meet with manager for injury updates, lineup notes and the latest on position competition.

12:30–1 p.m.: Media members congregate in lunchroom and are often regaled with stories from scouts.

1:05 p.m.: Find a seat in press box to view game.

2–3 p.m.: Head down to clubhouse to interview players who have been removed from the game.

4–5 p.m.: Return to press work room to file game story.

5 p.m.: Depart ballpark; return to hotel; meet colleagues for dinner. The day's news is often shared over meals.

SIGN THIS

FOR AUTOGRAPH SEEKERS, THERE'S PERHAPS NO BETTER TIME OF year than Spring Training. Having not faced a daily barrage of autograph requests all winter, players generally are more amenable to signing souvenirs than they might be during a heated pennant race.

The easier places to obtain autographs tend to be the older ballparks. At Dunedin Stadium in Florida, spring home of the Blue Jays, the only way for players avoid fans is to take an inconvenient detour through the field, so fans have a chance to interact with the athletes. Most of the older Arizona parks — Phoenix Municipal (A's), Tempe Diablo (Angels) and Scottsdale Stadium (Giants) — also offer fans a chance to mingle with their heroes.

The parks built in recent years provide players the utmost in privacy and convenience. In many newer facilities, players enter and exit the field via the dugout, much like they do during the regular season. Still, for autograph seekers patient enough to figure out the rhythms of a team's pregame routine, it's possible to go home with cherished signatures from Spring Training.

> *The design of the Astros' Oceola County Stadium is conducive to autograph seekers who set up in "Autograph Alley."*

The design of the Astros' Oceola County Stadium in Kissimmee, Fla., is conducive to autograph seekers, who set up in "Autograph Alley" — an area in the left-field corner where players pass to and from the field. Bradenton's McKechnie Field, another older classic facility, is also autograph-friendly.

Through the years, no spring facility was more popular with fans than Dodgertown in Vero Beach, Fla., home to the Dodgers franchise from 1948 through 2008. Because players had to walk through public areas to get almost anywhere, they tended to make signing part of their daily routine.

Autograph seeking began about the same time as Spring Training. In *Slide, Kelly, Slide*, the biography of Hall of Famer Mike "King" Kelly, author Marty Appel points to Kelly as the first sports figure to be approached for autographs. In the late 1880s, fans armed with pencils and scraps of paper walked with the popular Boston Beaneaters catcher as he made his way to the ballpark, hoping for a memento of their encounter. The sports memorabilia business exploded a century later, in the late 1980s, and players fielded a constant barrage of autograph requests, many from professionals looking to re-sell the signatures.

"It's tough sometimes," said Frank Thomas. "You try to be fair, and I think most guys recognize it as part of their job. It's really no big deal. But we all recognize that it's a big business now."

Players and veteran autograph seekers suggest collectors practice patience and limit their requests. Perhaps the biggest complaint among players is fans who keep coming back for more. Players who seem to be paying little attention can pick out familiar faces among the hundreds they see each day.

"You can tell," said Hall of Famer Tony Gwynn. "I didn't hit .300 all those years by not paying attention to things."

SIGN OF THE TIMES
Mets fans got acquainted with Carlos Beltran in 2005 when he took time to sign a few autographs during his first Spring Training with the club.

MURDERERS' ROW
Red Sox fans line up
for autographs at the
Ed Smith Complex i[n]
Sarasota, Fla.

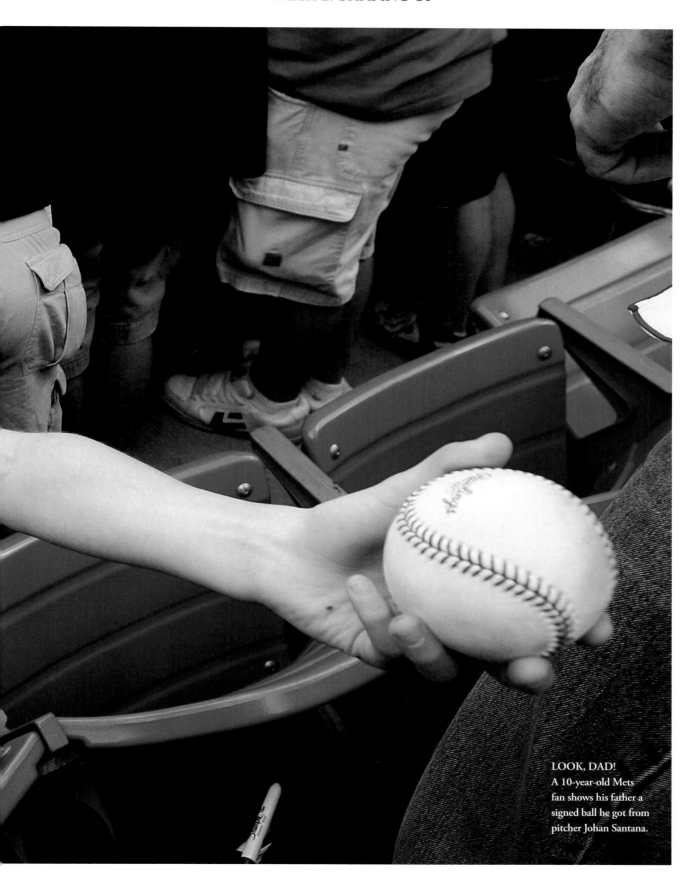

LOOK, DAD!
A 10-year-old Mets
fan shows his father a
signed ball he got from
pitcher Johan Santana.

WEEK 3: FUN AND GAMES

WITH ALL THE PLAYERS IN TOWN AND THE EXHIBITION SCHEDULE IN FULL SWING, this is when Spring Training really gets interesting. During the third week of camp, starting pitchers throw a couple of more innings per appearance and regulars last a little longer in the field. This is also when it's important for fans to pay extra attention to the players working out alongside the Big Leaguers, because celebrities like Billy Crystal and Bruce Hornsby start showing up at various camps. The real celebrity attractions, though, are baseball's living legends — Hall of Famers like Sandy Koufax, Yogi Berra, Al Kaline, Mike Schmidt, George Brett, Nolan Ryan and Dave Winfield — who provide instruction to the next generation of ballplayers.

The annual return of baseball royalty to the camps they inhabited as players isn't the only reunion taking place. Players who have switched teams via trade or free agency often see their former employers and fans for the first time. It's all part of the rhythms of spring, when everyone — and everything — begins anew.

TOUCHING THEM ALL The competition heats up during the third week, even when games are played on St. Patrick's Day.

BUILDING UP ARMS

FIRST-TIME VISITORS TO SPRING TRAINING ARE OFTEN STARTLED to see pitchers rotating through the games as if they were All-Star contests. Since there's nothing more precious to a Big League club than pitching, special care is taken during Spring Training to make sure that everyone from starters to closers is brought along slowly to help prevent injuries.

For starting pitchers, the goal for the first appearance in live action is usually 30 pitches, which amounts to about two innings. With each March start, a pitcher generally looks to throw 15 to 20 more pitches than the last outing, gradually building up to a six- or seven- inning workload of 90 to 95 pitches by the time the teams head north. All told, a starter will throw just 25 to 30 innings over the course of Spring Training.

> The increasingly strict pitch counts make it difficult to duplicate regular-season conditions. Pitchers and managers from previous generations believe today's pitchers are far too coddled, especially when it comes to the low number of pitches that they're allowed to throw.

"Spring Training is just to get a feel for your body," said right-hander Gil Meche. "I think the older I get, the smarter I get, trying not to push anything too hard during the spring."

Such a controlled process — one focusing on routine rather than results — works well for established players. But it's far more challenging for unproven pitchers to make an impression since they are rarely allowed to work through a lineup more than once. And even if they do stick around a game long enough, spring lineups often consist of players who are unlikely to make a Major League roster. Therefore, when it comes to making the team, veteran hurlers tend to have an advantage on making the club over younger pitchers. Not only have teams usually signed them to contracts, but the younger player usually has Minor League options left, which means that the organization can send him down without risking losing him to another Big League club.

This explains, at least in part, why the Minnesota Twins kept aging righty workhorse Livan Hernandez on the roster coming out of Spring Training in 2008 and sent down promising 24-year-old southpaw Francisco Liriano. It could also be considered a reason why Tampa Bay had top prospect David Price start the season in the Minors in 2009, even though he had dominated the Boston Red Sox in the 2008 ALCS.

Aside from being careful with young prospects like Price, the Rays are committed to pitch counts for all pitchers on the roster, even keeping veterans out of games for the first week or 10 days of spring exhibitions.

"I want these guys to be our guys for a long period of time," Rays Manager Joe Maddon said in 2009. "I know sometimes it runs counter to the conventional wisdom of the last 50 years or so, but that does not bother me." As fans have already seen, Maddon is a manager who views things through a different prism, and after his club's appearance in the 2008 World Series, many baseball people became willing to adopt his theories.

For relief pitchers, the Spring Training workload is similar to the regular season since they usually pitch just an inning every couple of days, racking up about 12 to 15 innings over the course of a March schedule. The goal, according to former Mets and Athletics pitching coach Rick Peterson, is for a reliever to have back-to-back appearances at least twice during the spring and appearances on three straight days at least one time.

Nevertheless, simulating game situations is a challenge even for relievers, since the order of pitchers is predetermined before each exhibition. A left-handed specialist might be scheduled to pitch the fifth inning and end up facing three right-handed batters. Closers typically are scheduled to pitch in the middle innings, when they'll face more Big League hitters, as opposed to those 20-year-old prospects playing in the ninth inning. But it's still hardly equivalent to a real late-inning save situation.

The increasingly strict pitch counts also make it difficult to duplicate regular-season conditions. Pitchers and managers from previous generations believe today's pitchers are far too coddled, especially when it comes to the low number of pitches that they're allowed to throw. As team president of the Texas Rangers, Nolan Ryan reportedly banned the use of pitch counts to determine how long pitchers stay in the game. The Hall of Famer — a tireless flamethrower as a player — implemented the policy during Spring Training in 2009, stressing that players need to focus more on conditioning and durability.

Hall of Famer Ferguson Jenkins believed in building up endurance during the spring and tried to throw at least two complete games before Opening Day. Just imagine such a notion in this decade. Jenkins says teams should at least bring back the practice of pitchers routinely throwing batting practice.

"You get back into the habit of seeing the ball off the bat and the reaction time of the hitter," Jenkins said. "I used to throw every second day, either on the side or BP. That's how I threw so many complete ballgames, because my arm was strong and that all starts in the spring. They have a different perception of what they have to do in the spring today."

ARMS RACE Francisco Liriano used Spring Training in 2009 to help build arm strength in hopes of avoiding arm injuries like the one he sustained in '06.

REUNIONS

Most players don't get a chance to say goodbye when they change teams. Whether through trade or free agency, most transactions come during the winter. Even if a move generates huge media coverage, with the player donning a jersey over a suit during an introductory press conference, the transition does not seem official until Spring Training.

Aside from giving new acquisitions a chance to meet their new teammates, Spring Training can also afford players the first opportunity to face their former teams, assuming they have remained in the same Spring Training league. When a player has switched teams after a long tenure in one city, the first meeting with his old club can be pleasant, albeit awkward.

In 2009, John Smoltz asked to make the two-and-a-half-hour trip with the Red Sox to Disney to face the Braves, even though he wasn't scheduled to pitch. Although he may have just wanted to get his first meeting with the Braves out of the way, it helped that he had a tee time with buddy Tiger Woods near the Braves' facility. Of course, the main reason was to visit with friends from the organization where he spent more than 20 years.

"I'll always be a part of the Braves," Smoltz said. "But for it to work for me, I've got to move on. Sometimes I get caught up in the 'us,' and that's a big mistake. You've got to remember not to make that mistake and allow guys to bust your chops. I used to do it with other guys."

Like Smoltz, Red Sox outfielder Jason Bay felt strange in '09 facing his former team during the spring, the Pirates, who had traded him to Boston the previous August.

"It's hard to just shut it off," Bay said of his ties to Pittsburgh. "You've been around them for five, six years — you've got friendships over there."

Rocco Baldelli's first trip to face the Rays during '09 Spring Training was especially emotional given his remarkable recovery from a career-threatening medical condition during the '08 season.

"I got more hugs today than I've gotten in a long time," said Baldelli, who joined the Red Sox prior to 2009. "It was nice to see everybody. I knew I'd get here and see all my buddies and say hello, and that's pretty much what it was. I've been in one place my whole career. This is the reality of the situation. I play for the Red Sox now. They're all still my friends, even though I'm competing against them."

Spring Training can provide players with the sendoff that they never got. Such moments also can help fans and players to turn the page, not that the organizations usually wait long. Baldelli, who wore No. 5 for Tampa Bay, became the first Red Sox player to wear the number since Nomar Garciaparra was traded in 2004. Pat Burrell, who wore No. 5 in Philadelphia, took Baldelli's number when he signed with Tampa. Garciaparra might have made it a three-way trade of No. 5, but opted to sign with Oakland instead of the Phillies.

Burrell, who had an up-and-down relationship with Philly fans, jumped at the chance to take the first Rays road trip to Clearwater, where he received a warm reception and realized, perhaps officially, that his decade in Philadelphia was over. "That's part of the business," Burrell said. "I'm not saying it's always easy, but that's part of it. Things happen for a reason. Fortunately, the relationship is good. I have nothing but good things to say about the organization."

P.F.P. TIME While getting used to his new environment in Red Sox camp in 2009 — the first time he didn't don a Braves uniform in 20-plus years — Smoltz takes part in the infamous "Pitchers' Fielding Practice."

TOGETHER AGAIN Nomar Garciaparra (right) catches up with former teammate Jason Varitek prior to a spring game in 2007. The pair played together in Boston for more than seven seasons and were college teammates at Georgia Tech.

LIVING LEGENDS

GEORGE BRETT WALKS BETWEEN THE FIELDS AT SURPRISE Stadium in Arizona, slapping backs, chatting up anyone within earshot and dispensing the occasional piece of hitting advice to players, many of whom were not even born when Brett was named American League MVP in 1980. He wears his familiar No. 5 Royals jersey and holds the title of vice president, but his main job is just being George Brett — a gig he is quite good at.

One morning in March 2009, Brett stumbled upon a group of collegiate baseball players from Kansas State University in town to play Arizona State, and he gave the youngsters an impromptu 15-minute address. Spotting one player wearing a Texas Rangers hat, he swiped it off his head and tossed it in a trash can, placing a new Royals hat on his head instead.

After continuing for several minutes, he pulled the hat out of the trash and returned it. "You can have this back," he joked. "Just don't wear it around here."

Baseball is the only sport in which Hall of Famers hold court almost every day during preseason camps, whether they work for a club or not. Yogi Berra and Reggie Jackson appear around the batting cage in Tampa. Bill Mazeroski is a fixture at the Pirates' camp in Bradenton. Mike Schmidt spends time with the Phillies in Clearwater, Al Kaline with the Tigers in Lakeland, and Lou Brock and Bob Gibson in Jupiter with the Cardinals.

Brett isn't even the only member of the Hall of Fame Class of 1999 roaming Surprise Stadium, not with the Royals sharing the complex with the Rangers and Team President Nolan Ryan.

Down the road at the Peoria Sports Complex, Dave Winfield shagged a few balls on a back field by himself — not giving instruction, just enjoying a workout.

"That's our new right fielder," San Diego Padres General Manager Kevin Towers quipped. "I hear that he's got good range and a pretty decent arm."

For retired players like Schmidt, who spent the 2004 season managing the Phillies' Class-A affiliate in Clearwater before returning to a life of golf and fishing, the Spring Training ritual provides an annual baseball fix. For those on team payrolls like Brett, Winfield and Jackson, suiting up during the spring is part of the job description.

Then there are players like Brock, who show up to Spring Training out of habit, their bodies still in tune with the rhythms of spring even 30 years after retiring.

"I love this more than anything," Brock said of his annual spring trip to Jupiter, Fla. "First, it's cold back home in St. Louis, and I can do without that. But mostly, I love what this all means to me. The sound of a ball hitting a glove — Pop! Pop! Pop! — is music to my ears. So is the crack of a bat. Those are sounds I'll never grow tired of. It's a symphony."

Although many Hall of Famers take a casual approach to Spring Training, they can make a major impact on current players just by talking with them, even those from other organizations. Veteran outfielder Cliff Floyd will never forget the time early in his career while he was playing with the Montreal Expos and Brock came to the Expos' facility in West Palm Beach and lectured on a back field about base stealing.

"A lot of us were fast but couldn't steal bases," Floyd recalled. "I thought it was pretty unbelievable how one of the best baserunners of all time could teach us young bucks how to steal a base. In our minds, we just take off and try to make it. There was technique to it, and you're learning from the master. Stuff like that only happens during Spring Training."

Frank White, the longtime Royals second baseman and coach who now works in the front office, said working with young players during Spring Training never grows old. "This is the fun part," he said. "I just stay out of everybody's way until they ask a question. You don't feel like you're working — you feel like you're helping, and that's the good part."

For some former players, serving as an instructor during Spring Training can be a way to dip a toe into coaching. That's how retired Yankees Ron Guidry and Don Mattingly made their entree into the coaching fraternity. Both ended up as full-time coaches for the Bronx Bombers during Joe Torre's time there as manager. "They took on more of a role in the spring than just being there to sign autographs and tell stories," Torre said. "Either way is fine. A lot of it is just continuing your ties to what made the history of the organization. It's pretty special to see these people around, whatever they want their role to be."

Through the years, few players have had more of a presence at Spring Training than Dodgers legendary ace Sandy Koufax. For years, before the club moved its spring home to Arizona, the reclusive Hall of Fame left-hander would quietly appear at the Dodgers spring camp in Vero Beach, Fla., to offer tips to both young pitchers and veterans. He also visits friends from other clubs and has become a regular guest at Mets camp in Port St. Lucie — just down Interstate 95 from Vero Beach — due to his ties with Mets Owner Fred Wilpon.

Padres Manager Bud Black — who pitched in the Majors for 14 seasons — recalled a spring as a coach with the Angels when Koufax showed up at the team's camp in Tempe, Ariz., to visit with Manager Mike Scioscia and coaches Mickey Hatcher and Ron Roenicke, all former Dodgers.

"I grew up a Giants fan with Willie Mays and Willie McCovey, but as a left-handed pitcher, I had always wanted to meet him," Black said. "We were in the clubhouse early, on stools talking baseball and my heart was just racing. Here I was, at 45 years old, and Sandy Koufax still had that kind of impact on me."

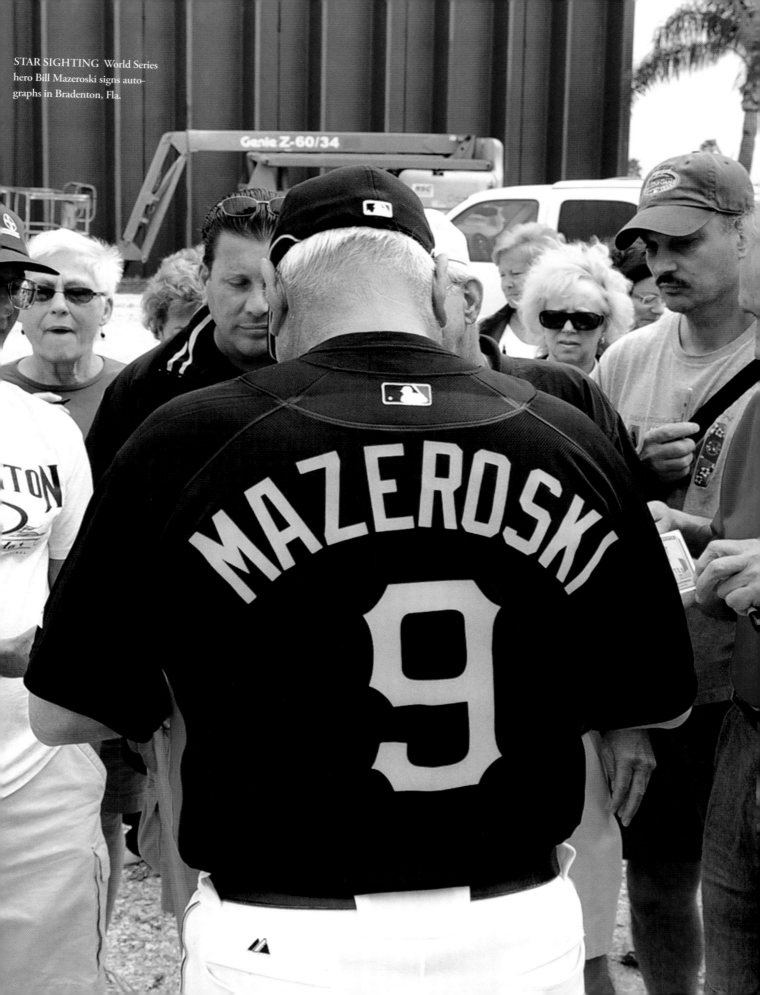

STAR SIGHTING World Series
hero Bill Mazeroski signs autographs in Bradenton, Fla.

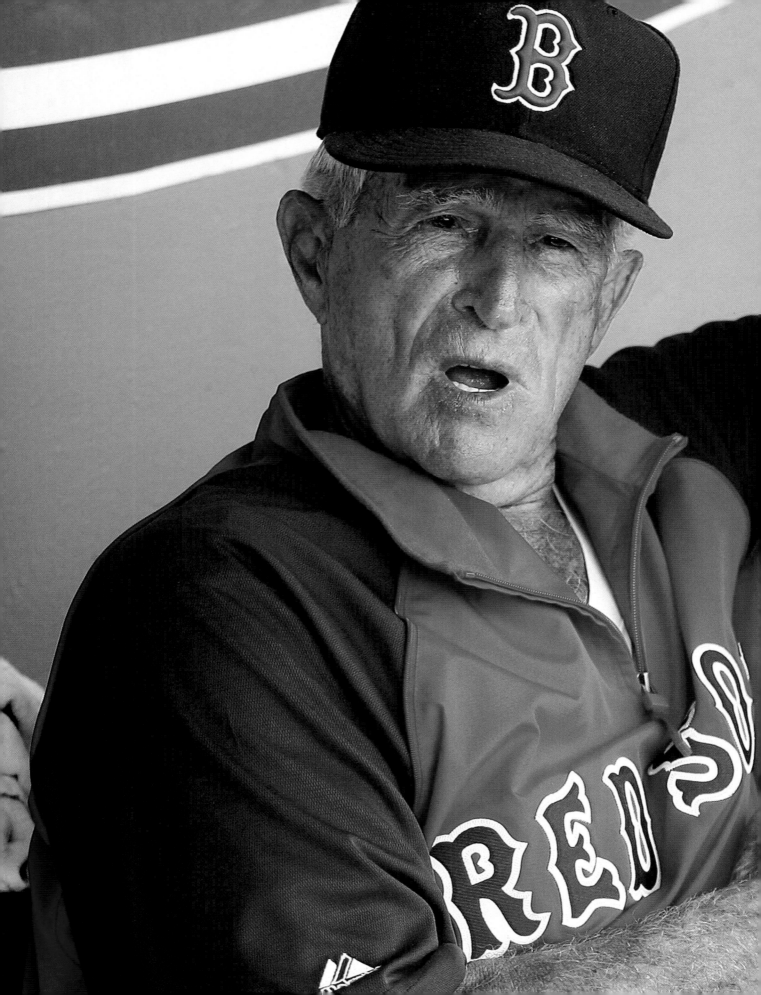

PASSING IT ON Boston legend Johnny Pesky, an infielder with the Red Sox during the 1940s and '50s, shares his wisdom and sense of humor with Dustin Pedroia.

GOING GREEN Fans can always count on seeing green caps and bases in March, as St. Patrick's Day annually falls in the middle of the Spring Training schedule.

IRISH SPRING

LONG BEFORE IT BECAME STANDARD FOR TEAMS TO WEAR GREEN UNIFORMS AND HATS ON ST. Patrick's Day, baseball had a long tradition of celebrating the holiday. According to Charles Fountain, author of *Under the March Sun*, players in the early part of the 20th century especially looked forward to the feast of Ireland's patron saint. Back then, many Big Leaguers had Irish ancestry. With St. Patrick's Day occurring during Lent, local bishops often gave dispensations from fasts and other commitments. Brooklyn Dodgers Owner Walter O'Malley threw lavish St. Patrick's Day parties at Dodgertown, with players, staff and writers celebrating together long into the night.

Such celebrations, though noteworthy, were off-the-record events. The Cincinnati Reds took baseball's St. Patrick's Day festivities public in 1978 when they donned green-and-white uniforms for a Grapefruit League game. Such garish threads soon became commonplace. Although the sight of the Big Red Machine in green was startling, the Reds had unwittingly created a Spring Training tradition. In 1981, the defending World Series champion Phillies broke out green uniforms, to the delight of reliever Tug McGraw. Since then, the Phillies have annually auctioned off their green hats for their ALS charity. The Boston Red Sox unveiled green hats on March 17, 1990, and added green jerseys in 2004. The Red Sox actually wore green more than once in 2007. Of course they donned the color in their Spring Training game in March, and then again on April 12, in honor of former Boston Celtics coach Red Auerbach, who died the previous offseason. With cool temperatures in Boston, several Red Sox players wore their normal red sleeves under the jerseys. Despite the odd Christmas look, the episode inspired several NBA teams to follow baseball's lead and wear green on St. Patrick's Day.

These days, virtually every Major League team wears green caps or jerseys or uses green bases for St. Patrick's Day. Some grounds crews stencil a shamrock onto the infield dirt or outfield grass. Even teams that don't don green for the day sell green merchandise at the souvenir stands.

DODGER GREEN The O'Malleys, Bavasis and Thompsons celebrate St. Patrick's Day at Dodgertown.

NO FASHION STATEMENT Green may not be their team's color, but these Tigers still enjoy getting into the spirit of St. Patrick's Day.

STAR POWER

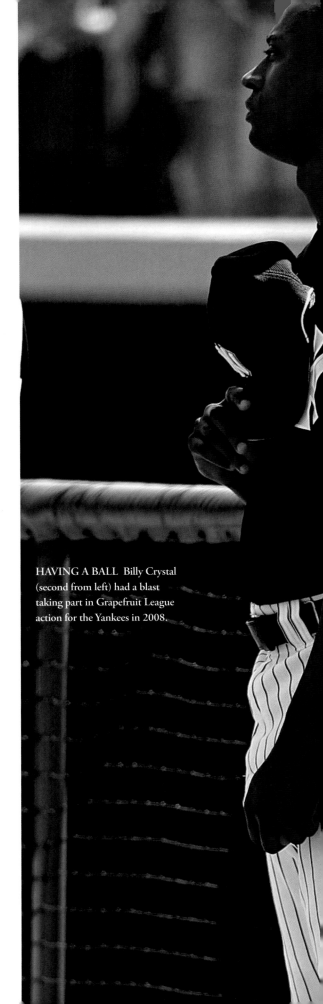

DURING THE REGULAR SEASON, TEAMS WILL OCCASIONALLY ALLOW celebrities and luminaries from other professional sports leagues to dress in uniform, take batting practice and otherwise be a part of the pregame atmosphere. Because of the laid-back nature of Spring Training, teams have on occasion taken such fantasy experiences a step further by allowing VIPs to participate in actual exhibition games.

In 1991, actor Tom Selleck spent time at Detroit Tigers camp in Lakeland in preparation for his movie *Mr. Baseball*. Late in the spring, the left-handed-hitting actor was sent up to face Tim Layana of the Reds, pinch-hitting for Rob Deer.

A record crowd of 7,210 fans at Joker Marchant Stadium rose and began cheering from the moment Selleck appeared in the on-deck circle. Layana threw a ball on his first pitch. Selleck then fouled a pitch behind the Reds' dugout on the third-base side, swung and missed a low and outside pitch, then hit a high foul into the left-field stands. Layana struck him out with a knuckle-curve.

"My knees were shaking a little bit," Selleck said after the at-bat. "He threw well, but he can probably throw a lot better. I pulled a hamstring a couple of days ago. I don't know what I'd have done if I'd have hit the ball. Probably hobbled to first."

In 1997, Angels Manager Terry Collins inserted Grammy-winning musician Bruce Hornsby as a pinch-runner for Kevin Bass with two outs in the seventh and his team ahead by three runs. Hornsby was left stranded when George Arias popped out to end the inning.

On March 13, 2008, actor and comedian Billy Crystal celebrated his 60th birthday a day early by leading off for the Yankees as the designated hitter against the Pittsburgh Pirates at George M. Steinbrenner Field. With fellow funnyman Robin Williams in attendance, and the capacity crowd cheering, Crystal strode to the plate in the bottom of the first. Taking the advice of teammate Derek Jeter to swing early in the count, Crystal fouled the first pitch — a fastball — from Pirates lefty Paul Maholm down the right-field line and got ahead in the count, 3-1, before striking out. Plate umpire Mark Carlson, who shook hands with Crystal before the at-bat, told him afterward that he had swung at ball four. "It was the strangest, greatest moment of my life," Crystal said.

Earlier in the day, the longtime baseball fan and director of the movie *61** took infield practice, jogged in the outfield with perennial MVP candidate Alex Rodriguez and talked around the batting cage with Hall of Famers Yogi Berra and Reggie Jackson. A day later, the Yankees "released" Crystal, who was listed as an infielder.

Other celebrities have spent extended periods of time in Spring Training, working with the ballplayers for weeks in order to raise their skill level and sometimes raise money for charity. Basketball legend Michael Jordan reported to the Chicago White Sox Spring Training camp in Sarasota in

HAVING A BALL Billy Crystal (second from left) had a blast taking part in Grapefruit League action for the Yankees in 2008.

A TALL ORDER At White Sox camp in 1994, basketball legend Michael Jordan found that his swing wasn't always as sweet as his jump shot.

1994 in an attempt to launch a baseball career. He spent a month with the Big Leaguers, playing in spring exhibitions, before being assigned to Minor League camp.

Jordan had rocked the sports world in 1993 by announcing his retirement from the NBA. Already having led the Chicago Bulls to three consecutive NBA championships and capturing seven individual scoring titles along the way, Jordan announced a few months after the retirement news broke that he was returning to his first love — baseball. And that seems to be the common thread among many of these celebrities who join the Grapefruit and Cactus League action at various times of life: They all really dreamed of being a *baseball player*. Spring Training happens to be the unique time of year when they can slip into a dugout, grab a bat and maybe even face a 90-mph fastball.

Some celebrities have also found ways to raise funds and awareness for charities while fulfilling a lifelong dream of their own by joining Major League training camps. Take country music star Garth Brooks, who spent four Spring Trainings raising money for his Touch 'em All Foundation. Brooks joined the San Diego Padres in Peoria, Ariz., in 1998 and '99, going 1 for 22 at the plate in '99. In 2000, he shifted to Mets camp in Port St. Lucie, Fla., but didn't register a hit in 17 at-bats. He took a few years away from the sport but returned with the Kansas City Royals in '04.

Some baseball purists might suggest that the celebrities make a mockery of the game and keep Big Leaguers from taking the exhibition games seriously. Padres General Manager Kevin Towers, though, notes that Brooks participated in every last drill and conditioning session. Towers said that Brooks also taught the players a few valuable lessons about being a professional entertainer.

"Garth really helped our players realize how important fans are," Towers said. "When you saw one of the top entertainers in the business sitting out there in the dark signing every last autograph, it was good for our players to see that. They had a greater appreciation for why this guy had such a huge following. It didn't matter who it was, he would not leave the parking lot until he signed every last autograph.

"Here's a guy as popular or more popular than any player that we've ever had, and to watch him interact with people was incredible. The way he communicated with his fans and the way he approached Spring Training — first one here, last one to leave. Whatever you asked of him, he did. He wanted no special treatment. What a great memory."

> rdan announced a few months after
> e retirement news broke that he was
> turning to his first love — baseball.
> nd that seems to be a common thread
> mong many of these celebrities who join
> e Grapefruit and Cactus League action
> t various times of life: They all really
> reamed of being a baseball player.

TOUCH 'EM ALL FOUNDATION

It's every kid's dream to have professional athletes in his corner. Country music star Garth Brooks enables every child to have just that. In 1999, Brooks established the Touch 'Em All Foundation, one of several divisions within his expansive Teammates for Kids Foundation, a non-profit organization that partners with elite athletes to raise money for children's causes.

Brooks co-founded Teammates for Kids with Bo Mitchell, a former player in the St. Louis Cardinals organization. Baseball was the first sport represented by the charity. Over the years, athletes from professional hockey, football and soccer clubs have also teamed with Brooks to assist children in need. In 2009, the foundation expanded to include a fifth basketball division, with the help of NBA athlete Chris Paul. Other notable members of Brooks' lineup include his former Padres teammates Tony Gwynn and Wally Joyner, as well as standouts Albert Pujols, David Wright and Kevin Youkilis.

Athletes who team up with Brooks pledge to contribute a pre-arranged dollar amount for each hit, goal, touchdown or other statistical mark that they attain throughout the season. Pitchers may donate $100 per strikeout, while hitters may pledge a gift of $1,000 for each home run they belt. Hockey players may offer $200 an assist, and field goals may garner $500 each. Touch 'Em All then triples the amount bestowed by the athletes before donating the money.

Brooks tackled fundraising for Touch 'Em All in a unique way during its inaugural year and several subsequent seasons. Instead of receiving a salary for his Spring Training stint with the Padres, Brooks contracted with the team to be paid $200,000 — the equivalent of Major League Baseball's minimum player salary at the time — in the form of a donation to his charity. These funds, along with those generated by the athletes, have been used to champion Little League Baseball's Challenger Division as well as other programs emphasizing children's health and education.

Brooks

SKIN CANCER SCREENINGS

EVEN IN MARCH, THE SUN CAN BE INTENSE IN FLORIDA AND Arizona, especially between the hours of 10 a.m. and 3 p.m., when fans are watching workouts and games. As another unique part of Spring Training, fans that have gotten too much sun exposure over the years can be screened for skin cancer prior to some Grapefruit League games. Baseball Commissioner Bud Selig, himself a skin cancer survivor, has been instrumental in raising awareness.

"I'm proud that baseball is a leader in the fight against skin cancer," Selig said. "The next generation of field personnel and the next generation of fans will be smarter and safer when it comes to the sun."

Major League Baseball and the MLB Players Association joined with the American Academy of Dermatology in 1999 to create the "Play Sun Smart" Skin Cancer Awareness Program. In that time, the partners have used a unique and effective approach to raise awareness of sun-safe behaviors and skin self-examination.

"Since 1999, the baseball community has helped to educate its fans about the importance of sun-safe behavior by getting screened for skin cancer and encouraging the public to conduct regular skin self-examinations to look for signs of skin cancer, which can be successfully treated if caught early," says dermatologist C. William Hanke, the AAD president.

Aside from MLB's "Play Sun Smart" campaign, individual clubs have also been working to educate fans about skin cancer. Notably, the Tampa Bay Rays have teamed up with the Moffitt Cancer Center.

SPRING CHEMISTRY

A MAJOR LEAGUE CLUBHOUSE IS A LARGE-SCALE CHEMISTRY experiment. A general manager assembles players he hopes will form a competitive team, but also possess the elusive "clubhouse chemistry" that often defines championship contenders.

That chemistry often develops during Spring Training. In February 1993, reliever Mitch Williams took a look at the wacky personalities assembled in the Phillies clubhouse in Clearwater and remarked, "We went out and got more gypsies, tramps and thieves."

That wild bunch of Phillies — which included Darren Daulton, John Kruk, Lenny Dykstra and a young Curt Schilling — swaggered its way to a National League pennant.

In an attempt to foster team chemistry in the New York Yankees' Spring Training clubhouse, Manager Joe Girardi called off a late-February workout in 2009 and took the team on a short bus trip to a pool hall. Aside from giving the players a well-deserved break, it also enabled them to get to know one another away from the ballpark.

Throughout Bobby Cox's managerial tenure with the Braves, the team has taken its calm professional approach from stars such as Tom Glavine, John Smoltz, Greg Maddux and Chipper Jones. Whether in West Palm Beach or more recently at Disney's Wide World of Sports, Braves veterans have used their common interest in golf and shared belief in hard work to set the tone for the newcomers.

"You see that every spring," said Cox. "They're having fun, but they get their work done. Younger guys see that, and it makes a difference."

Tony Gwynn, perhaps the most approachable star the game has ever known, occupied a corner locker near the entrance to the Padres clubhouse at the Peoria Sports Complex, arriving early each day and setting the tone for the team with his hard work and pleasant demeanor. Closer Trevor Hoffman maintained a similar disposition as he took on the leadership role after Gwynn's retirement.

Likewise, the low-key atmosphere in the Blue Jays Spring Training clubhouse in Dunedin, Fla., has long been defined by veterans Vernon Wells and Roy Halladay, two of the more unassuming All-Stars in the game. "You have to get along because you're going to spend so much time together," Wells said. "I think what happens in Spring Training from a chemistry standpoint is probably almost as important as what happens on field."

In 2008, the Rays brought in veteran professionals such as Cliff Floyd and Troy Percival. The chemistry difference was immediately apparent in Spring Training, and was touted as one of the reasons for the team's remarkable turnaround. "Usually you can tell by Spring Training if a team is going to click," said Floyd, who played for three different playoff teams from 2006–08. "When you see guys laughing in the clubhouse, having a good time, that's usually a good sign."

RALLYING POINT
When the competition on the diamond is done for the day, Tigers Minor Leaguers sometimes bond by getting fired up over table tennis.

FOCAL POINT Barry Zito checks out the view from the other side of the camera at a 2005 Spring Training photo shoot.

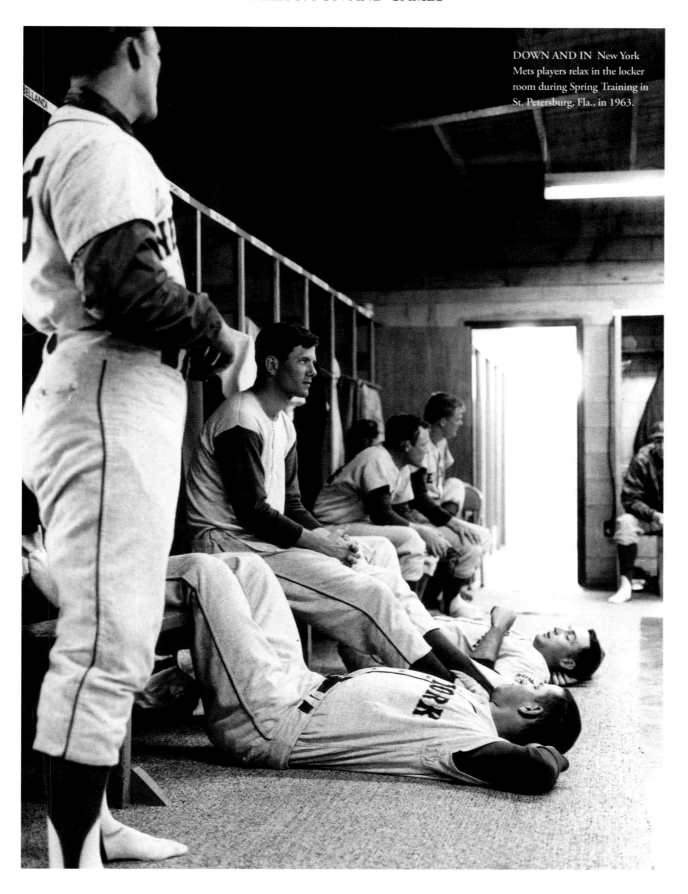

DOWN AND IN New York Mets players relax in the locker room during Spring Training in St. Petersburg, Fla., in 1963.

WEEK 4: DIVERSIONS

A VACATION TO ARIZONA OR FLORIDA DURING SPRING TRAINING PROVIDES A CHANCE to do more than just enjoy America's pastime. The Grand Canyon State and Sunshine State are two of North America's most popular tourist destinations, especially in February and March, when most states are still dealing with the last cold spells of winter. Whether it's Florida's breathtaking beaches, sunsets, fishing or kitschy "Old Florida" attractions; or Arizona's red rocks, desert scenery and outdoor adventures; there's no shortage of diversions from the ballpark in each Spring Training locale. It's possible to go to Disney World in Florida or see one of the Seven Wonders of the World in Arizona. The sites surrounding both the Cactus League and the Grapefruit League facilities offer world-class golf and dining, along with enough warm weather to make visiting fans wish they could relocate permanently. It's no wonder that so many Big Leaguers do just that.

HOOP DREAM Players also enjoy life off the field in Spring Training — Joba Chamberlain got to shoot hoops before a 2009 Orlando Magic game.

FISHING CHARTERS

FOR MANY BASEBALL FANS, AS WELL AS MANY BALLPLAYERS, A SPRING visit to Florida isn't complete without a fishing trip. Retired pitcher Doug Creek made fishing excursions as much a part of his spring as long toss and infield drills. As a reliever for seven Big League teams from 1995 through 2005, he spent many a Spring Training afternoon on the water, especially when he played for Tampa Bay from 2000–02.

These days, Creek is a licensed captain operating Doug Creek Charters out of Punta Gorda, Fla., a short drive from the Rays' spring home at Charlotte Sports Park and an hour's drive from Fort Myers, the spring home of the Red Sox and Twins. Creek takes two or four passengers out at a time on his 24-foot boat for trips ranging from a half-day to a full day. During March, fishermen in this part of Florida are most likely to catch redfish and snook. The area is known for world-class tarpon fishing, too, but that season doesn't begin until May, when most players — and fans in town for Spring Training — have returned north.

Since trading the rosin bag for a reel, Creek has taken Rays players and front-office staff on fishing charters — Troy Percival caught a whopping 38-inch snook in 2009. Some of the folks who hire Creek know him as part of the cast of the local reality show *Tarpon of Boca*, which has aired on The Outdoor Channel, and only learn their captain was a Major Leaguer once they are out on the water. But some do book him because of his baseball experience.

"It sort of continues the theme of their baseball vacation," Creek said. "I'm always happy to tell stories from my playing career and keep people entertained, but the main goal is to catch some fish and have a good time."

THE CATCH

It has become a rite of spring for many baseball players to cast their lines in the hopes of reeling in some big fish during Spring Training. Forget charter buses and planes — these players want charter fishing boats.

For many guys, like Doug Creek, Jason Isringhausen and Troy Percival, you often need to look no further than Florida's Charlotte Harbor to find them. "There's a brotherhood among ballplayers if they're going to go fishing," said Creek. "They can come out and spend a day on the water, and they can get away from their celebrity a little bit."

Big League hurlers Josh Beckett and Brad Radke have had fishing ingrained in them since youth.

"I started when I was old enough to hold the pole, about 4 or 5 years old, and I haven't stopped since," said Radke, a former Twins hurler. "It's just a mad craze. When I was 10 or 11 years old, I really started to fish a lot. It's just relaxing to me."

R&R TIME (from left) Yankees Mickey Mantle, Bob Grim, Billy Martin and Whitey Ford on a spring fishing trip.

LITTLE GUYS Yogi Berra spends time fishing with two of his sons during Spring Training.

TEE TIME

When it comes to playing golf during Spring Training, the Atlanta Braves set a high standard during the 1990s. Throughout the decade, the Braves' "Big Three" pitching trio of Greg Maddux, John Smoltz and Tom Glavine played golf virtually daily, completing as many as 45 holes after morning workouts. The trio was together from 1993 through 2002, with at least one of the future Hall of Fame pitchers remaining with the team at all times through 2009 Spring Training. Other teammates have been equally passionate about golf through the years, including third baseman Chipper Jones and outfielder Jeff Francoeur.

"I encourage it," longtime skipper Bobby Cox said at one point. "It's a great way of getting their mind off of problems. It would bother me if they *didn't* play golf."

The Atlanta Braves' pitchers began hitting the links together when the club trained in West Palm Beach, Fla., and were thrilled when the team moved to Disney's Wide World of Sports complex in 1998, which is closer to more world-class golf courses. Although the pitchers also fished together on a regular basis during Spring Training, golf was always a little easier to fit into their schedule.

Smoltz, who has a 1.6 handicap and hopes to compete on the PGA Champions Tour one day, has played regularly with buddy Tiger Woods, whose primary residence for many years was at the Isleworth Golf & Country Club in Orlando. Jones recalls a memorable afternoon when he and Smoltz played 36 holes with Woods, LPGA star Annika Sorenstam and infielder Adam LaRoche at the Reunion Resort.

"That was an experience, probably the best tutorial round of golf I've ever had in my life," Jones said. "I learned more from Tiger and Annika that year than I've learned in the rest of my life on the golf course."

Jones shot well that day, but could only manage a 76, 13 strokes behind Woods. Smoltz edged Sorenstam by two strokes with 68, while LaRoche shot a 73.

"I was really trying to compete hard against Annika," Smoltz said. "And on the first tee Tiger said, 'I'll bet she beats you.' We all played from the same tees. And she was super nice."

TEEING OFF AROUND DISNEY

Braves players and personnel don't have to go far to hit the links when they need an escape from their February and March drills. Luckily for them, there are four championship-caliber courses on the 35-square-mile Disney property where the club's camp is located. The Magnolia and Palm courses host the PGA Tour Children's Miracle Network Classic, the final event on the PGA Tour schedule.

The Disney property also includes the town of Celebration, a planned community developed in the 1990s that includes the Celebration Golf Club. The Ginn Reunion Resort, just a few miles from the Braves' complex, also has three golf courses, each designed by a golf legend: Arnold Palmer, Jack Nicklaus and Tom Watson. Because convenience matters, many Braves rent homes at the resort for the spring.

Jeff Francoeur tried to play whenever he could during his time with the Braves, especially when he had the opportunity to play with Tiger Woods, who always seems willing to shoot a round with pros from other sports.

"I've learned so much from him about the mental side of golf," Francoeur said. "It's so true that he's one of the most mentally tough guys. He can turn it on and off when he wants to. The first time or two, you just kind of play and talk, and he's great. He gives you strokes. But if you start beating him, he won't give them to you anymore."

FORE! Like many players, Paul Molitor (left) and Robin Yount relax by taking part in a round of golf during Spring Training in 1990.

TAKING CUTS
Giants players watch
GM Carl Hubbell take
a swing at the Casa
Grande facility in
Arizona in 1967.

VALLEY OF THE SUN

IF GREATER PHOENIX OFFERED ONLY SPRING TRAINING BASEBALL, THAT WOULD BE enough to attract hordes of fans in the months of February and March. While much of the country is still blanketed in snow, the average high temperature in Arizona during the month of February is 70 degrees. Hospitable weather and even more welcoming locals were two of the reasons why legendary baseball owner and promoter Bill Veeck moved the Cleveland Indians' spring camp to Tucson for 1947. At that time, clubs held their training camps mostly in the southeast, with a few based in the west. With 330 days of sunshine per year, the Southwest proved a perfect backdrop for Spring Training and would eventually grow to an equal stature with Florida when it came to hosting preseason training for Big League clubs.

Unlike in Florida, there's little danger of a rainout in Arizona's "Valley of the Sun," which includes Phoenix, Scottsdale, Tempe and Mesa, along with other communities such as Peoria, Surprise, Maryvale and Goodyear. The latter four cities were put on the map largely by landing Spring Training baseball. Located on a flat desert basin amid scattered, barren rocky mountain peaks, the valley has blossomed over the last decade, fueled by the perfect storm of business growth, a real estate boom and tourism. Yet the area still retains a small-town feel. Many people who have lived in Phoenix for decades find it hard to imagine that their quiet home has become such a popular tourist spot, attracting a whopping 13 million annual visitors to the desert oasis. People come from around the globe to relax and regenerate, mostly by playing golf, unwinding at world-class spas and enjoying the panoramic scenery. They also come, of course, for the baseball. Aside from Spring Training, the Grand Canyon State is also home to the Arizona Fall League, which showcases some of the game's top prospects each autumn shortly after the conclusion of the World Series.

TAKE ME OUT Don & Charlie's — covered in sports artifacts — is popular among fans and insiders.

CHICAGO WEST
When it's March in the Phoenix area, it usually means that many Chicagoans have temporarily relocated to Arizona to follow their beloved Cubs.

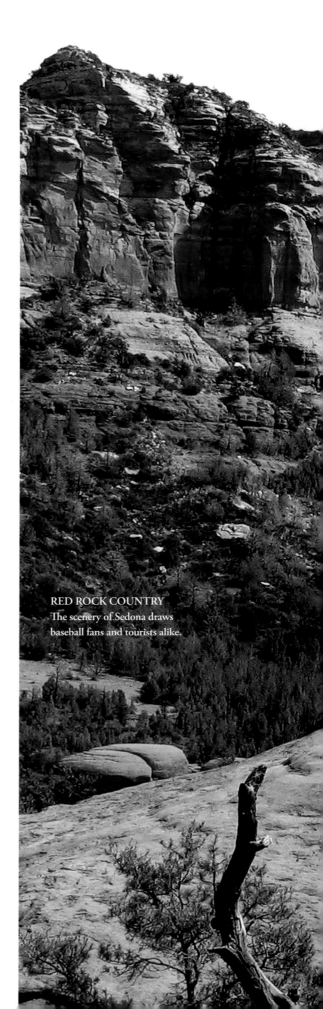

Amidst the browns, beiges and reds of the Arizona landscape the influx of Cubbie Blue can be quite noticeable in the spring. During March, it often seems like the entire city of Chicago has relocated to the Phoenix area to root for the Cubs. The Cubbies were one of the earliest teams to settle in Arizona. First moving to Mesa in 1952, they've been at their current Mesa facility — Hohokam Park — since 1979. Like many teams that have been around for a while, the Cubs first trained in some places that today would seem bizarre. They called Catalina Island, Calif., their spring home for two decades starting in the 1920s, and the club even trained in French Lick, Ind., for three years during the '40s.

Without much of a downtown hub in Phoenix, it can be tough for sightseers to know where to begin. Many first-time visitors head directly for the red rocks of Sedona, two hours to the north of Phoenix, or even further afield to the Grand Canyon. Greater Phoenix has certainly developed around its mega-resorts, such as The Arizona Biltmore Resort & Spas and The Phoenician, not to mention the upscale resorts in the north Scottsdale region of Gainey Ranch. Phoenix itself showcases some of the most beautifully manicured lawns, golf courses and resorts in the country. Few areas offer as many ways to explore, whether via hot air balloon, Jeep tour, hiking — with the most popular trek being to the top of Camelback Mountain — biking, horseback riding or mountain climbing.

Although downtown Phoenix — with fewer restaurants and shops than places like New York and Miami — lacks the get-out-and-walk feel of many cities across the nation, it has grown by leaps and bounds in recent years, aided by the opening of the baseball stadium now known as Chase Field, home to the Arizona Diamondbacks. Thanks to the D-backs, Phoenix hosted a World Series, which Arizona won over the Yankees in 2001, and the city was selected to host the 2011 MLB All-Star Game. Baseball fans will definitely want to visit Don & Charlie's restaurant in Scottsdale. Decorated from floor to ceiling with sports memorabilia, it's a popular gathering spot for players, baseball executives, celebrities and media types.

Downtown Phoenix also has no shortage of can't-miss non-sports attractions, such as the Phoenix Art Museum. Tops on the list for most visitors is the Desert Botanical Garden, which displays more than 20,000 desert plants from around the world. It's adjacent to the Phoenix Zoo; the downtown Heard Museum, one of the nation's best museums of Native American culture; and Taliesin West, built by Frank Lloyd Wright in 1937 as a winter retreat. (The buildings now serve as the headquarters of the Frank Lloyd Wright Foundation and School of Architecture.)

Whether visitors make the trip to town for baseball or backpacking, there are numerous things to do indoors and out in the Valley of the Sun, and the area is working hard at becoming even more accommodating to visitors who make the trek to picturesque Arizona.

Located on a flat desert basin amid scattered, barren rocky mountain peaks, the valley has blossomed over the last decade, fueled by the perfect storm of business growth, a real estate boom and tourism. Yet the area still retains a small-town feel.

RED ROCK COUNTRY
The scenery of Sedona draws baseball fans and tourists alike.

CAN'T BEAT THE BEACH
The sun sets over Bradenton Bea

A BALL BY THE BAY

TAMPA BAY — THE AREA LOOSELY-DEFINED AS TAMPA, ST. Petersburg, Clearwater and numerous smaller communities — is technically down to just three Spring Training teams: the Yankees (Tampa), Phillies (Clearwater) and Toronto Blue Jays (Dunedin).

The Tigers (Lakeland) and Pirates (Bradenton) also can be considered in the Tampa Bay area since growth in the last decade has made Polk and Manatee counties bedroom communities for the nation's 18th largest media market. Even with just those teams, Tampa Bay's combination of baseball, beaches, golf, restaurants, festivals and amusement parks makes it a perennial favorite.

When there are no games to watch, fans can head to one of numerous beaches in the Tampa Bay area to soak up some sun. Stephen Leatherman, a.k.a. "Dr. Beach" has ranked the nation's top 10 beaches since 1991. Two of Tampa Bay's beaches have won the No. 1 honor. Fort DeSoto Park's North Beach in St. Petersburg, not far from Tropicana Field and Al Lang Field, won in 2005. Caladesi Island Beach, a 15-minute drive from Dunedin Stadium, won in 2008. Both are public parks featuring long stretches of unspoiled, white-sand seashore, free of development and noise.

If hitting the links is the goal, TPC Tampa Bay is located in Lutz, just north of Tampa. The Innisbrook Resort & Country Club in Palm Harbor is especially popular with Phillies and Blue Jays players.

For fishermen, Tarpon Springs is a quaint fishing village just north of Dunedin. It's home to one of the largest populations of Greeks outside of Greece, and it's also where slugger Pat Burrell owns a home.

While a trip to Florida often leads to thoughts of Disney World in Orlando, Tampa Bay has plenty to offer thrill seekers, whether it's the roller coasters and animals at the safari-themed Busch Gardens, the Adventure Island water park, the Lowry Park Zoo or the Florida Aquarium, all located in Tampa. Nearby St. Petersburg is home to Derby Lane, one of the top tracks in the country for greyhound racing. Derby Lane has baseball ties all the way back to the early 1900s, when Babe Ruth, Lou Gehrig and Stan Musial were regulars at the track.

When talk turns to food, Bern's Steakhouse in South Tampa certainly lives up to its billing as one of America's finest spots. For casual fare, grab a grouper sandwich at The Hurricane on St. Pete Beach or at one of the four Frenchy's locations on Clearwater Beach.

Once a major cigar manufacturing district, Ybor City is now Tampa Bay's most popular nightlife destination, with restaurants, bars and shops lining Seventh Avenue. Not as raucous as Bourbon Street in New Orleans, especially during weeknights, it's a great place to grab dinner and people-watch. Plant City, the spring home of the Reds from 1988–97, located just east of Tampa, is best known for hosting the Florida Strawberry Festival the first two weeks of March.

A FIXTURE The Tigers have called Lakeland, Fla., home since 1946, the longest-running relationship among Big League Spring Training sites.

HAPPIEST PLACE ON EARTH

THE ATLANTA BRAVES NO LONGER NEED TO WIN THE WORLD Series to go to Disney World. They have reported there each February since 1998. The Braves' Champion Stadium anchors Disney's Wide World of Sports, a sprawling 220-acre complex of playing fields, gyms and field houses. The multi-use complex hosts roughly 200 events a year across 40 sports, attracting thousands of kids and adults.

The complex has had ties to baseball since it opened. An All-Star team of MLB players trained there prior to a November 1998 tour of Japan. After the 1998 season, it also hosted the Players Choice Awards. The Orlando Rays, the Double-A affiliate of the Tampa Bay Rays, played at Champion Stadium from 2000–03. More recently, Champion Stadium hosted World Baseball Classic games in 2006 and a regular-season series for the Rays in 2007 and '08. During Spring Training, groups of football players training for the NFL scouting combine use the Braves' weight room. On weekends when the Braves are hosting spring exhibitions, there's usually a youth volleyball, basketball, cheerleading or gymnastics event next door at the "Milk House" fieldhouse. "There's always something going on," said Braves Manager Bobby Cox. "I can't keep track of it all."

Disney officials say the complex wouldn't have been possible were it not for the Braves, whose fans enjoy perhaps the most elegant Spring Training park in baseball. The stadium is immaculate and features several huge gift shops packed with Braves merchandise.

For families looking to combine baseball and theme parks into one vacation, the Disney-Braves connection makes it easy. For Braves players looking to visit Disney, Universal Studios or other theme parks with their families, it couldn't be more convenient. Theme parks typically offer VIP programs: For an additional fee, a personal guide is arranged for pro athletes and their families, allowing them to skip lines and have extra security, if needed. That fee sometimes is waived if the player agrees to do some publicity for the amusement park, which can be as simple as posing for pictures with costumed characters.

Braves slugger Chipper Jones, who grew up in Florida, says he's past the point of visiting theme parks, letting his wife take the kids while he's training. But being a huge marine biology enthusiast, he's always up for a trip to SeaWorld. "I've always been fascinated by sharks, whales and dolphins," Jones said. "So every spring I make it a point to go over and check them out at least once."

WORLD SPOTLIGHT Disney's Champion Stadium hosted World Baseball Classic games — held during Spring Training — in March 2006.

BASEBALL SCHOOL

During February and March, students at Curtis Fundamental Elementary can't help but pay attention to Spring Training. That's because the Florida school is adjacent to Dunedin Stadium, spring home of the Toronto Blue Jays. It's the only school in Florida or Arizona so close to a spring complex — home runs hit to left- and center-field land in the schoolyard.

"There's an air of excitement whenever the Jays have a game," said Principal Kathy Duncan. "You can hear the crowd noise, smell the hamburgers and even see parts of the field from certain angles."

On game days, students can hear music coming from the ballpark as early as 10 a.m., but Duncan says the Jays are sensitive to the students and keep the volume down, especially during a week-long period of standardized testing in mid-March. Many classrooms have a view of the grandstand. To catch a glimpse of the game during recess or gym classes, students will stand on picnic tables or peer through gaps in the fence, creating a "knothole" experience.

Duncan says students grow accustomed to having Spring Training baseball literally in their backyard, although there tends to be more buzz when the Jays are playing the Yankees or hometown Rays. Since exhibitions typically begin at 1 p.m. and school dismisses at 2:15, there's little disruption to traffic flow, although signs must be posted to keep fans from parking on school property.

The school campus consists of a number of buildings, all of which are at least 100 feet from the outfield wall. No home run ball struck the school in 2009, although it's within the realm of possibility, especially for a right-handed dead pull hitter. "You'd have to really get a hold of one," says Jays outfielder Vernon Wells. "I don't think the school has anything to worry about."

BASEBALL AND BOOKS

Curtis Elementary School opened in the 1920s and pre-dates the Toronto Blue Jays, who have trained in Dunedin, Fla., since their inception in 1977. The public school teaches children from kindergarten through fifth grade and was previously known as Dunedin Elementary. After a year of extensive remodeling and expansion, the facility reopened in the fall of 2008 as Curtis Fundamental Elementary.

Curtis Fundamental, ironically, had been located in Clearwater not far from Jack Russell Stadium, home to the Philadelphia Phillies until 2004, when the team moved to the new Bright House Networks Field.

In Clearwater, the school was not nearly as close to baseball as it is in Dunedin, where teachers and students retrieve balls hit into the schoolyard, which, of course, they're free to keep. Once Spring Training ends, officials from the Jays' affiliate in the Florida State League give students a behind-the-scenes tour of the ballpark.

MOONSHOT Even during spring cuts at Dunedin
Stadium, the Curtis Fundamental Elementary school
(beyond the left-field fence) is just about out of reach

SOUVENIRS When Buckley's tour stops in Scottsdale, Ariz., fans can pick up Spring Training souvenirs.

BASEBALL TOURS

For many baseball fans, Spring Training is about driving leisurely through Florida or Arizona, making up the itinerary along the way. For other fans, though, the idea of taking a pre-arranged group tour is more appealing. To make things easier for those spring travelers who prefer it, the hotel rooms, game tickets and ground transportation are included in many pre-packaged Spring Training tours. All the fan has to do is get to Arizona or Florida.

Jay Buckley has been taking baseball fans on Spring Training tours for more than a decade as part of his "Jay Buckley Baseball Tours," which also offers week-long trips to various Big League ballparks during the regular season. Each March, Buckley's tour company takes about three dozen fans to Arizona and the same-size group to Florida, usually during the last two weeks of Spring Training when managers begin to field lineups composed almost exclusively of players who will head north.

In Arizona, the tour stays at a hotel in Scottsdale's Old Town neighborhood. The historic district is within walking distance of the Giants' Scottsdale Stadium, as well as The Pink Pony and Don & Charlie's — two of the most popular restaurants among past and present baseball players, executives and fans. In Florida, the tour stays in Orlando and, of course, features more bus travel. Buckley designs the trip to hit as many ballparks as possible. One day on the Florida tour might feature an afternoon game at Bradenton's McKechnie Field and an evening tilt at Steinbrenner Field in Tampa. Or perhaps an afternoon game at Disney World featuring the Braves and an evening affair at the Tigers' Joker Marchant Stadium in Lakeland.

The trips offered by Buckley typically last 10 to 12 days. Less time is spent on the bus in Arizona, where all but two parks are located within an hour's drive of Scottsdale; the tour generally doesn't hit Tucson. With so much baseball — and driving, in the case of Florida — packed into the schedule, there's little time for sightseeing, although Buckley tries to piggy-back some stops onto the drive-time wherever possible.

In Tampa, for instance, the tour barely has to veer off course to hit several prominent baseball sites. After exiting Interstate 275 onto Dale Mabry Highway, the tour passes the Yankees' Minor League training complex, where Major League players often come to rehab injuries during the regular season. Just north of that is Raymond James Stadium, home to the NFL's Tampa Bay Buccaneers which was built on the site of Al Lopez Field, the spring headquarters for the Chicago White Sox from 1957–59 and the Cincinnati Reds from 1957–87.

Al Lopez, the Tampa native and Hall of Fame catcher and manager, also is the namesake of Al Lopez Park, a tree-lined recreational area just northeast of Steinbrenner Field. Also nearby is Jesuit High School, a private all-boys school whose alumni include Lopez as well as former Major Leaguers Lou Piniella, Brad Radke and Dave Magadan.

"We do sightseeing as we go, giving everyone the history of the ballparks and the areas as we go through them," Buckley said. "We don't just give them a key to the hotel room and a ticket."

The tickets Buckley provides to his travelers are choice seats, usually between home plate and third base, about 10 to 20 rows from the field. The tour usually makes stops at 13 parks in Florida, generally catching the Red Sox, Twins and Orioles when those clubs are on the road since they reside in the southern-most reaches of the Sunshine State. Buckley begins plotting the itineraries in early December, once the spring schedules are released. Although he hosts fans of all ages, even some from Europe, most of his clients tend to be older folks with flexible schedules. Buckley can relate. Before retiring as a middle school principal, he restricted his baseball business to regular-season tours in the summer. Now the spring tours are among his most popular.

"I like comparing all of the different parks and seeing the players close up," said Chris Peters of Cedar Falls, Iowa, who took a Florida tour in the spring of 2009. "I'm fine with keeping it almost exclusively baseball. You can go to Disney any time."

PACKED HOUSE
Always one of the more popular facilities, the Yankees' George M. Steinbrenner Field is an exciting stop on any fan's tour of Spring Training sites in Florida.

WEEK 5: DOWN TO THE WIRE

THE NONCHALANT ATTITUDE DURING EARLY SPRING TRAINING GAMES BEGINS TO change in week five. With jobs on the line and Opening Day creeping closer, camps take on a more serious tone. Players who crammed together at lunch tables during the first weeks of Spring Training keep more to themselves; there's more space, after all, with the first rounds of cuts having been made. Exhibition contests start to resemble regular-season affairs, with managers playing their regular lineups and starting pitchers inching closer to 90 pitches in each outing. Games continue to start at 1 p.m. for the most part, but teams begin playing in some 7 p.m. starts to simulate the regular season. Look closely during the fifth week of camp and it's possible to see torches being passed, with veterans secure in their legacies mentoring up-and-coming players who seem likely to make the club, passing their knowledge to the next generation of stars.

NIGHT OWLS The Dodgers take on the Mariners in a sight that becomes more common late in Spring Training — a night game.

ROUNDING INTO FORM

THE FIFTH WEEK OF SPRING TRAINING IS USUALLY WHEN CLUBS MAKE THE SECOND-TO-LAST round of roster cuts, often involving the last spots off the bench or in the bullpen. It's an awkward time in the clubhouse as the players — who often know each other from the Minors or previous Big League stops — compete for roles while being forced to interact in tight quarters. The friendly banter of February disappears as the reality of the competition for jobs comes into focus near the end of March.

The action on the field is also changing as dramatically as the demeanor behind the scenes. Fans that bemoaned Minor Leaguers getting Big League playing time in early March are treated at the end of the month to lineups that look mostly like those that will be used in April. Even the clubhouse looks more like the norm, with the roster whittled to 30 or fewer players. After a few weeks of camp, those who are left are beginning to look as focused and tired as they do during the regular season.

"During the first couple of weeks, guys are joking on the bus and talking," said Braves Manager Bobby Cox. "By the end, they're asleep as soon as we're out of the parking lot."

It's not that the players are exhausted; nobody would ever mistake Spring Training for a rigorous NFL preseason camp. But by the fifth week, players are adjusting their biological clocks to the unusual sleep patterns of the regular season. The schedule helps, with most teams playing more 7 p.m. games.

"Spring Training should be all night games; after all, you're preparing for the regular season," said veteran closer Troy Percival. "The last week or two you see a lot of night games and that helps you get used to the transition."

The shift to night games doesn't come early enough for some players. "I like to sleep," said Blue Jays starter Dustin McGowan. "Getting up early every day is tough for me."

Regardless of the game time, starters are now aiming for 90 pitches over six innings each time they take the hill, which, given the modern emphasis on pitch counts, is practically a full outing. This rigid pitch count helps managers map out their pitching rotations through the month of April. The challenge is to make sure each of the five starters is getting enough work to reach the 90-pitch milestone. Sometimes a team will send a Big League starter to pitch in a Minor League game if there aren't enough innings to go around in the contests between Big League teams.

In Minor League games, conditions can be controlled. If a veteran pitcher exceeds his pitch count without retiring the side, his team could simply request to end the inning. Such games can also produce some amusing situations, like when 45-year-old Randy Johnson squared off in 2009 against a lineup composed almost exclusively of players half his age. Although teams always have ways of getting work for their frontline players, it can be tough for a spot starter or middle reliever on the bubble to get much playing time during the fifth week.

With the five starters, the closer and set-up men usually determined at this point, the final roster decisions can come down to which players have Minor League options left. Teams are reluctant to part with older players already signed to guaranteed contracts as well as those without options who will be claimed by another club if placed on waivers.

"We try to go on stuff and makeup as much as anything else, but sometimes contracts have a lot to do with it," admitted *Chicago Cubs Manager Lou Piniella*.

Nobody would ever mistake Spring Training for a rigorous NFL pre-season camp. But by the fifth week, players are adjusting their biological clocks to the unusual sleep patterns of the regular season. The schedule helps, with most teams playing more 7 p.m. games.

BACKGROUND
Even though games grow more intense, the scenery — like at Tempe Diablo Stadium in Arizona — reminds all that it's still Spring Training.

FULL SPEED AHEAD
The intensity picks up as Spring Training progresses, with players giving it their all as the competition for jobs grows more fierce.

RUN IN THE SUN
Diamondbacks players
work themselves into top
condition during Spring
Training in Tucson, Ariz.

SPRING MEMORIES

PERHAPS IT'S THE PICTURE-PERFECT SCENERY, THE BALMY WEATHER or the universal optimism, but for some reason Spring Training produces some of the best memories for baseball players, whether they break camp with the Big League club or not. The 2000 AL MVP, Jason Giambi, can still remember his early Spring Training days with the Oakland A's, his locker next to veteran pitchers Dave Stewart and Rich "Goose" Gossage and two stalls down from legendary closer Dennis Eckersley. All-Star Nomar Garciaparra recalled playing shortstop for the Red Sox during his first camp and robbing the Twins' Kirby Puckett of a hit.

"I remember him yelling at me from across the field in a friendly way, just getting on me for taking away a hit," Garciaparra said. "I thought that was pretty cool. Here I am, a young kid, and Kirby Puckett already is sort of accepting me."

Padres General Manager Kevin Towers' most memorable spring moment came in 1996 after he signed Hall of Famer Rickey Henderson. Baseball's greatest leadoff man was known for arriving late to Spring Training, and Towers, who had been unable to reach Henderson, wasn't sure when his mercurial left fielder might show up.

"We had never had any big-name free agents, so this was a big deal for us," Towers recalled several years later. "We were kind of biting our nails wondering when he was going to show up; he's not the easiest guy to get a hold of. So he comes into the clubhouse at 7 in the morning and announces, 'Rickey is here,' and the place just erupts. He really added some electricity to the clubhouse."

Hall-of-Fame hurler Ferguson Jenkins thinks back fondly to Spring Training in 1974 at Pompano Beach, Fla., his first with the Rangers after being traded by the Cubs following a disappointing '73 campaign in which he posted a 14-16 record and lost more games than he won for the first time since his first full season in '66. Some thought he was washed up. Rangers Manager Billy Martin approached him on the first day of Spring Training and asked if the rumors were true.

"I said, 'Skip, you give me the ball every fourth day and I'll win you some games," Jenkins said.

The hard-working Jenkins knew that he had found a match with Martin, who at times was known for burning out pitchers. That season, Jenkins posted career highs in wins (25) and innings (328.1) while throwing 29 complete games. With Martin's help, Jenkins proved that reports of his demise were premature. The 6-foot-5 right-hander followed up his stellar '74 campaign with 85 more wins over the next six seasons. Every Spring Training, there are moments when a player tells his new manager what he's all about, just as Jenkins informed Martin that March.

Anyone who played for the Diamondbacks or Giants in 2001 has no problem coming up with his most memorable Spring Training moment. In the seventh inning of a contest between NL West rivals at Tucson Electric

RICKEY'S HERE Padres GM Kevin Towers was nervous that Rickey Henderson might not show up to camp in 1996, but he did — and he put a charge into the Padres' clubhouse.

Park, D-backs hurler Randy Johnson unleashed a 90-plus-mph fastball as a dove flew in front of home plate. The ball struck the bird, which was knocked over catcher Rod Barajas's head and landed a few feet from the plate amid a cloud of feathers. The footage of Johnson's heater colliding with the ill-fated bird still plays endlessly on sports highlight shows around the country even though the pitch came in a game that didn't count.

"I'm sitting there waiting for it, and I'm expecting to catch the thing, and all you see is an explosion," Barajas said. Even though the catcher had yet to play a full season in the Major Leagues, he unwittingly became a part of one of the more infamous plays in Spring Training history.

"Every so often, you'll be hitting fungoes from both sides [of the field] during batting practice and the balls will hit in mid-air," said former Diamondbacks Manager Bob Melvin, a coach for the team in 2001. "But I never saw anything close to that."

Aside from players seeing things they had never seen before, Spring Training gives some ballplayers their only chance to play in front of their hometown fans. For players who grew up in Arizona and Florida, playing in a Spring Training game for the first time can be every bit as thrilling as making a Big League debut.

Doug Waechter grew up in St. Petersburg, Fla., watching the St. Louis Cardinals each spring at Al Lang Field. In 1999, Tampa Bay drafted him in the third round. The following spring, he got to pitch at Al Lang Field.

"Growing up there and seeing that place, you got a special feeling just taking the mound in downtown St. Pete with all of that history and atmosphere," Waechter said. Of course, pitching at Al Lang was a dream come true for the young Waechter. But in 2003, things got even better for the right-hander when he made Tampa Bay's 25-man roster and got the opportunity to pitch in a Major League regular-season game at Tropicana Field, which is also located in St. Petersburg.

Blue Jays pitcher Jesse Litsch, a Pinellas County native like Waechter, attended Spring Training games in St. Petersburg, Clearwater and Dunedin as a youngster, and worked as a home clubhouse attendant for Tampa Bay at Al Lang Field in 2001 and '02.

"I would miss a couple of days of school here and there, but mostly just my last-period class," Litsch said. "I'd leave after lunchtime, and I actually got school credit for it for a class that involved on-the-job training. Those are things that kids up north just never get to experience."

Anyone who played with the D-backs or Giants in 2001 has no problem coming up with his most memorable spring moment. In the seventh inning of a D-backs win at Tucson Electric Park, Johnson unleashed a fastball just as a dove flew in front of home plate. The ball struck the bird, which landed a few feet from the plate amid a cloud of feathers.

READY OR NOT In 2001 Spring Training, Randy Johnson's heater got attention for a unique reason — it hit a bird.

SNEAK PEEK A fan steals a free look at pregame warmups before a spring game at Space Coast Stadium in Viera, Fla.

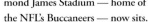

DOWNTOWN TAMPA
Al Lopez Field opened in 1955 in Tampa at the location where Raymond James Stadium — home of the NFL's Buccaneers — now sits.

SPRING ICONS

BUILT AT A COST OF $287,901, AL LOPEZ FIELD OPENED ON MARCH 10, 1955. In its first game, the Chicago White Sox beat the Cincinnati Redlegs, 10-7, on a grand slam by Minnie Minoso before a crowd of 3,025. The White Sox — managed by Tampa's own Al Lopez from 1957 through 1965 and again in 1968 and '69 — shared the facility with Cincinnati before bolting for Sarasota in 1960. The Reds stayed another three decades. Pete Rose and Johnny Bench were among the Reds stars that played as Minor Leaguers at Al Lopez Field for the Tampa Tarpons of the Florida State League.

Al Lopez Field may not have been around for as long as some of the other iconic Spring Training ballparks, but it sure hosted its share of memories — and big-time players. Lopez may have been the first Tampa native to become a prominent Big Leaguer, he was far from the last. Numerous future Major League All-Stars grew up in Tampa, including Lou Piniella, Steve Garvey, Gary Sheffield, Dwight Gooden, Wade Boggs and Fred McGriff — who resided just four blocks from Al Lopez Field.

When asked to name his favorite memory of the former Spring Training park, Lopez recalled an argument with umpire John Stevens.

"He said, 'One more word out of you, and you're gone,'" Lopez recalled. "I said, 'You can't throw me out of this ballpark. This is *my* ballpark — Al Lopez Field.' He said, 'Get out of here.' He threw me out of my own ballpark."

Like Al Lopez Field, "Baseball City," the Spring Training home of the Kansas City Royals from 1988–2002, was also the preseason home to some great ballplayers, such as George Brett, Frank White, Willie Wilson and a young Bo Jackson.

With Interstate 75 not yet extended down the west coast of Florida, three-hour trips to and from the club's previous complex in Fort Myers were routine, and Royals players and personnel were overjoyed at the change.

"There used to be times where we had to leave before the sun came up, be three hours on the bus, play a three-hour game, then spend another three hours going back on the bus," recalled Braves President John Schuerholz, the Royals' general manager at the time. "Six hours on the bus and you arrive again in the dark. We really couldn't get much work done."

In its heyday, Baseball City was a state-of-the-art complex nestled in the heart of the Grapefruit League. It was adjacent to a theme park that figured to lure casual baseball fans away from Orlando's Disney World and Tampa's Busch Gardens. For a brief period, Baseball City flourished and became a popular stop on the Grapefruit League tour. ESPN even taped a trivia game show on the site in 1988 and 1989. The short-lived show featured three-person teams of college students and was hosted by a young Chris Berman.

Despite the initial excitement, there are no remnants of Baseball City today in Davenport, Fla. The complex was demolished to make way for Posner Park, a combination residential and retail development.

DODGERTOWN

Holman Stadium, by modern standards, isn't much of a stadium. But then again, Dodgertown isn't exactly a town. But with a past almost as rich as the game of baseball itself, it's hard not to recognize the lure of this historic Spring Training venue that once hosted Dodgers legends Jackie Robinson, Gil Hodges, Roy Campanella and Sandy Koufax. From the day Dodgertown first opened in 1953 until the final inning was played on March 17, 2008, its doors were never shut. In fact, there weren't any doors, or dugouts, or anything other than a chain link fence separating some of baseball's greatest from 6,500 spectators. Beloved Dodgers Manager Tommy Lasorda was even said to have conversed with many in the first row of stands as he managed the Dodgers from their home bench.

Easily the most accessible of Spring Training sites, the Grapefruit League's Dodgertown was the home of both the Brooklyn and Los Angeles franchises for more than 55 years. The $100,000 stadium remained largely unchanged until 1984, when the original steel chairs from Brooklyn's Ebbets Field were replaced. In 2008, after more than half a century of loyalty to its preseason home, the club left Dodgertown — the last western team to grace Florida's Spring Training fields — for Arizona.

DODGERTOWN FACTS:

• Seating capacity: 6,474
• Rows of seats: 17
• Construction Cost: $100,000
• Size of the complex: 220 acres
• Location: Vero Beach, Fla., on the site of a former U.S. Naval Air base
• Architect: Norman Bel Geddes, designer of the Futurama building at the 1964 New York World's Fair
• Named for Bud Holman, a local business owner who persuaded the Dodgers to move to Vero Beach, Fla.
• The only privately owned Big League training camp in the country

UP CLOSE Fans were able to get very close to the action at Dodgertown — close enough to feel a Derek Lowe pitch breeze by in the bullpen.

COMMUNITY Dodgers coach Manny Mota often rode a bicycle from one end of Dodgertown to another.

STEP RIGHT UP Fans at the ticket window at Dodgertown's Holman Stadium prior to a 2008 Spring Training game.

THE PUPIL As a rookie in Dodgers camp in '06, Chad Billingsley found a friend and mentor in veteran Aaron Sele.

ROOKIES & MENTORS

SPRING TRAINING IS OFTEN THE TIME WHEN THE TORCH IS passed from veterans to promising rookies, when apprenticeships develop on back fields late in the afternoon or in the clubhouses in the wee hours of the morning. A's Manager Bob Geren was in his first Spring Training in 1980 after the Padres drafted him in the first round in 1979 when All-Star Dave Winfield invited him to dinner at the Yuma Country Club. Winfield, himself a former first-round draft pick of the Padres, picked the 18-year-old Geren up in a fancy car and used the dinner to prepare the youngster for the Big Leagues.

"He asked me how far from the plate I stood and I said I didn't know," Geren recalled. "He told me exactly how far and back his feet were, the length and direction of his stride and how important that was. He stressed that baseball is a big business and you have to know everything about it if you want to be successful.

"It's like a lawyer preparing for a case; you have to know everything. Baseball is fun and you're supposed to have a good time, but you better know your craft from every angle. I think that talk got me on the road to becoming a manager. A Spring Training dinner in Yuma 30 years ago; it's funny what makes a difference in your life."

For Yankees captain Derek Jeter, such a moment came in 1995, the team's final spring in Fort Lauderdale, Fla., and what would be the last spring camp for then-captain Don Mattingly. The respected veteran and the top prospect finished a workout one afternoon alone on a back field. Some of their teammates were playing an exhibition game while others were done for the day. Jeter and Mattingly headed back to the clubhouse with no fans, coaches or players around.

"Let's run in," Mattingly told Jeter. "You never know who's watching." It's clear from Jeter's relentless play and classy demeanor over the next decade that he took the advice to heart.

During one of second baseman Orlando Hudson's first springs with the Blue Jays, coaches George Bell and Ernie Whitt worked with him extensively on his hitting from both sides of the plate, no doubt recognizing the promise of the young infielder.

"I remember George Bell wearing me out in the cage," Hudson said. "He and Ernie Whitt — every day, morning and afternoon. I said, 'Are you serious about this?' Obviously they saw something."

Many newer spring facilities house all of the organization's Minor League players in close proximity to the Big League camp, creating a natural environment for mentoring. In the late '90s, Alex Rodriguez was not far removed from his rookie season when one morning at the Mariners' Spring Training complex in Peoria, Ariz., he was approached by several Minor Leaguers around the batting cage. Rodriguez invited them to dinner, offering to drive them if they met him outside the Mariners' clubhouse that evening. When Rodriguez showed up, he found 27 Minor Leaguers waiting. Rather than begging off, Rodriguez enlisted the help of teammate John Marzano and together they shuttled the youngsters to a nearby restaurant where the famished — and grateful — ballplayers ran up an $1,100 dinner bill.

Brian Roberts was surrounded by some All-Star talent in his first springs with the Orioles, where he picked the brains of veterans, like Cal Ripken, Jeff Conine, B.J. Surhoff and Scott Erickson.

"I was fortunate to be around guys like that early on and realize what it took to play at this level," he said. "If you look at most successful players, I'm sure you'd find that to be the case."

Pitcher Chad Billingsley remembered being a little intimidated during his first Big League training camp with the Dodgers in 2006. The clubhouse was filled with veteran players he had watched as far back as junior high school, such as Derek Lowe, Nomar Garciaparra, Jeff Kent and Eric Gagne. Billingsley found a friend and mentor in journeyman pitcher Aaron Sele.

"He really helped me out," Billingsley said. "I learned a lot from him, not just about pitching, but also what it's like in the Big Leagues, and how to carry yourself."

For Tony Clark, his initial Big League Spring Training in Lakeland, Fla., was an intimidating experience. Even at 6-foot-7, 260 pounds, he felt scared and uncomfortable around such Detroit Tigers veterans as Kirk Gibson, Cecil Fielder, Lou Whitaker and Eric Davis.

"I was scared to death," he said. "I remember sitting in camp with my head literally in my locker, not looking to make eye contact or hold conversations with anybody. The guys were on me constantly. But it was one of those things I found out later that if they had been quiet, they wouldn't have had much hope for you."

Chad Billingsley remembers being intimidated during his first Big League training camp with the Dodgers in 2006. The clubhouse was filled with veteran players he had watched as far back as junior high school, such as Derek Lowe, Nomar Garciaparra, Jeff Kent and Eric Gagne.

WEEK 6: NORTHBOUND

THE SIXTH AND FINAL WEEK OF SPRING TRAINING IS PERHAPS THE LEAST COMfortable time of the baseball season, both physically and emotionally. Players dress in clubhouses that are crowded with boxes, luggage and golf clubs, as clubhouse staff prepares for moving day. Tension is thick, as fringe players await word on whether they have made the team. With so much going on internally, teams stay close to home during week six, facing only opponents in closest proximity. Even after clubs depart Arizona or Florida, Spring Training isn't quite over. Many teams will face an unusual opponent in an unusual place during the final weekend before Opening Day. These detours allow fans in Las Vegas to see the Cubs and Mariners, or Memphis fans to catch the White Sox and Mets. It's the time when the Red Sox might face the Dodgers … in the Los Angeles Coliseum. It can be a hectic end to an otherwise leisurely six weeks of Spring Training, a kickstart to the marathon regular season.

CUT TIME Cubs Manager Don Zimmer watches a spring game in 1991, knowing that he has some tough roster decisions to make.

HOMESTRETCH

FOR MANY MAJOR LEAGUERS, SPRING TRAINING IS THE MOST PLEASANT TIME OF THE YEAR, a time to fit in a few easy workouts between tee times and fishing trips. For managers and coaches, it's a peaceful time, the only part of the season in which they're no worse off than any other team in the Big Leagues. Don't tell them that all those overused Spring Training metaphors of hope and renewal are cliche — those feelings are really in the air in February and March.

Amidst all of this calm, the last week of Spring Training can also be unrelentingly stressful for some players. For them — the aging veteran trying to hang on, the journeyman looking for yet another temporary gig, the not-so-young-anymore Minor Leaguer trying to break into the Majors — each morning brings the possibility of being released, or at the very least getting sent back to the Minor Leagues.

The early Spring Training honeymoon ends by the first week of March — well before the final days of the preseason set in — as players start getting released and reality sets in. Clubhouse personnel quickly clean out the lockers of the departed, both to lessen the embarrassment for the released player, and to keep the remaining "bubble" players from dwelling on it. The tension mounts as the weeks go by. Players must perform their best amid such anxiety, which reaches a peak during the sixth week of camp when final roster moves are made. Fringe players keep to themselves. There's little joking and laughter. Many ballplayers avoid talking to the press, not wanting their quotes to be misconstrued by management.

"It's the longest seven days of the year," said journeyman catcher Gregg Zaun, who shuffled around much of his career before settling down in his mid-30s with the Toronto Blue Jays. "It wears on you mentally after a while because all you want to know is where you're going to be, and where you're going to live.

"It's especially tough for pitchers and catchers because you've arrived a week earlier than everyone else, and you're dragging."

With as many as 65 players crammed into clubhouses in mid-February, it's no secret that Spring Training, for all the talk of clean slates and laid-back workouts, is a brutal war of attrition for those on the fringe. And the battle gets more intense as April approaches. So while fans kick back in the stands, slathered in sunscreen with beer in hand, and veterans secure in their jobs leave for the golf course after dutifully playing a few innings as a minor tune-up, the rest of the players in camp continue an agonizing wait.

Rex Hudler, the Los Angeles Angels' colorful broadcaster and former journeyman utility player, spent most of his 21-year professional career dreading those late-March mornings when the danger of being cut was highest. One of the most gregarious men in all of baseball, Hudler still can't bring himself to go into clubhouses in late March even years after retiring.

"I went through it so much as a player that I can't bear to relive that tension and anxiety," Hudler said. "You can just feel it in the air. For a lot of guys, it's a question of how they're going to pay the next month's bills. What about the house and health coverage? I was on that bubble almost every year, and even though there's not a day that goes by that I don't think about playing, that's one thing I will never miss."

Hudler, as evidenced by the fact that he played in the Major Leagues for parts of 13 seasons, put together a respectable career, especially for someone who felt that "the Turk" was going to come knocking on those late-March mornings to send him home. He batted .261 for his career, which ended in 1998 as a reserve player for the Phillies. And, contrary to the belief of many, Hudler proved that at times Spring Training statistics really do matter, as they're often a precursor of things to come.

In 1996, for example, Hudler batted .328 in 58 exhibition at-bats, throwing in three home runs for good measure. During that year's regular season with the Angels, he batted .311 with 16 home runs, both career highs by a landslide.

ESSING A 13-year
jor Leaguer, Rex Hudler
ually felt anxiety about
king the Major League
ad out of Spring Training.

ALL OUT As teams break camp, they often play a series in a unique locale, like this 2008 game in Las Vegas between the Cubs and the Mariners.

THE NUMBERS GAME

MOST TEAMS HAVE FEWER THAN FIVE OPENINGS ON THE 25-man regular-season roster during Spring Training, but clubs still bring in dozens of additional players on the off chance that someone with immediate value has slipped through the cracks. Perhaps a player has made a remarkable recovery from surgery or been coaxed out of retirement. There's the occasional player who jumps from Single-A or Double-A to the Majors, or the free-agent veteran pitcher who unexpectedly finds his way onto the roster because of injuries. For some veterans, Spring Training is particularly tough because it forces them to face the looming reality of retirement before the season even begins. Others report to preseason camp knowing that they have only a modest chance to play another year, but they want to enjoy one last spring or, at the very least, leave on their own terms.

Seven-time All-Star Tim Raines arrived at Yankees camp in Tampa in 2000 after missing most of 1999 with lupus, a chronic inflammatory disease. He surprised some by announcing his retirement during Spring Training even though it looked like he had a reasonable shot at making the club.

"I had a good career, but the fire wasn't there anymore," Raines said at the time. "I came back because the doctors had told me that I couldn't play again, but I proved to myself that I could. At least that way, there's no unfinished business."

Apparently there was. After sitting out the 2000 season, Raines came back and played for the Expos and Orioles in 2001 and for the Marlins in 2002. He played in just four games in 2001, then batted .191 in 89 at-bats in 2002. But Raines didn't come back to pile up numbers; it was about going out on his own terms.

For a Hall-of-Fame-caliber player like Raines, who played into his 40s, the end of a career is not as stressful as it is for less accomplished players just trying to stay in the Majors into their early 30s.

"You put your ego aside as you get older and you come to the realization that this is what you've got to do," said right-handed reliever Brandon Duckworth, who came to Royals training camp in 2009 as a non-roster player.

Having to accept an invite as a non-roster player is one of many humbling experiences that a veteran might endure during Spring Training. It's also common for teams to release a veteran to make way for a rookie, both for the upgrade in talent and for financial reasons. And while a bad spring will hurt a player's chances of making the team, a good showing sometimes will make little difference.

Younger players battling for roster spots have slightly less to worry about during the spring because they can be sent back down to the Minors more easily, and are under far less pressure to earn a Big League roster spot. If they make the team, their Major League careers begin earlier. If not, they're going back down as expected. Veterans, meanwhile, are fighting for their baseball lives.

In past generations, before cost became a factor in every personnel decision, clubs would usually keep an older player based on experience. These days, though, many teams will go with a younger player because he's less expensive. That puts more pressure on the veterans to perform in the spring. Then again, financial considerations can cause some teams to send a top prospect down to the Minors at the close of camp to keep his Big League service time from starting, postponing his eligibility for salary arbitration and free agency.

In 2008, top third-base prospect Evan Longoria of the Rays had a monster spring only to be sent down to Triple-A Durham when the season began. Skeptics wondered if the Rays' motivation was to keep Longoria's clock from ticking toward arbitration and free-agent eligibility. A year later, the Rays sent down top prospect David Price after a similarly impressive spring. In both instances, the Rays said the players needed more seasoning, and called them up early in the regular season.

As pitching coach for the well-heeled Yankees, Dave Eiland has the luxury of knowing that cost is generally not an issue when it comes to roster decisions. If anything, he has fewer decisions to make since the Yankees have long-term contracts with many of their pitchers. During his 10 Big League seasons, Eiland posted a 12-27 record and started 15 games or more just once, making him another prime example of a player who never quite knew for sure that he would earn a Major League roster spot. As a former on-the-bubble pitcher for the Yankees, Padres and Rays during his career, he's sympathetic to what some players are going through in late March.

"You're going to think about it; it's only human nature," Eiland said. "But if you think about it too much, it will drive you crazy. I just came in every day, got my work in and pitched the best I could. After that, it was out of my hands."

Spring Training, ironically, might be the toughest time for a fringe player to earn a spot on a team since established players are the healthiest and roster deficiencies are not as apparent before the grind of the regular season begins.

"It's always tough to look a veteran in the eye who has a true passion for the game and who has done everything you've asked him to do in Spring Training," said Chuck LaMar, the Phillies assistant GM for player development and scouting who spent eight years as general manager of the Rays. "They'll ask, 'Why did you even bring me in here?' And sometimes there is no good answer other than that your needs changed.

"But the silver lining is that if they've played that well in the spring, they'll get a chance somewhere else. I told every guy I released that they couldn't make our club right now, not that there wasn't a spot in the Major Leagues somewhere for them."

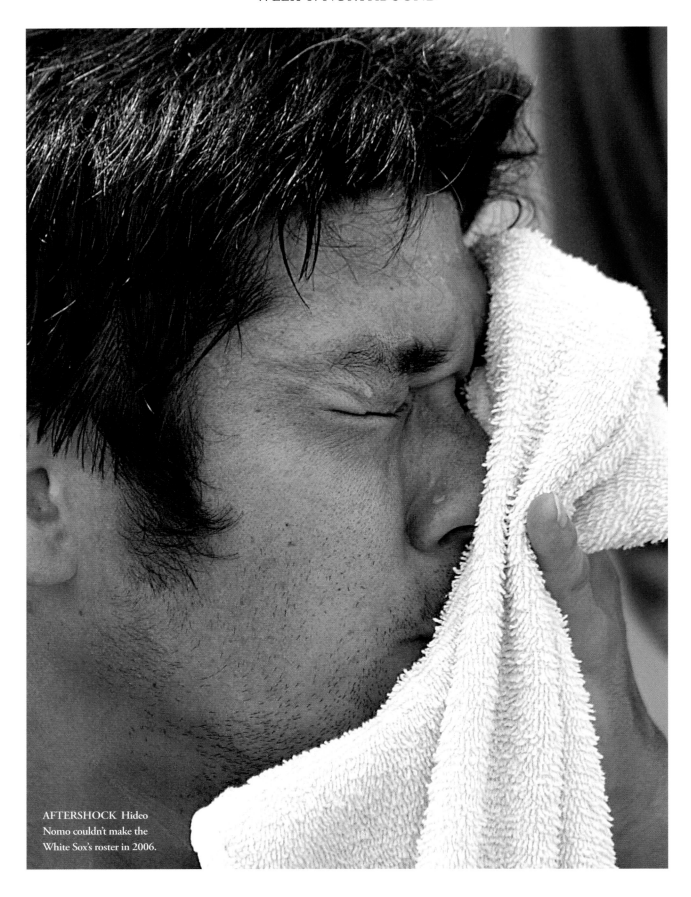

AFTERSHOCK Hideo Nomo couldn't make the White Sox's roster in 2006.

FINAL CUTS

THE LAST WEEK OF SPRING TRAINING IN 2007 WAS A DIFFICULT one for first baseman Carlos Pena. Already a veteran of four Big League teams at the age of 28, he was in a battle to land a reserve role on his fifth club, this time in Tampa Bay. Pena hit .214 that spring, with just four RBI in 42 at-bats, and lost the final roster spot to another journeyman, Greg Norton. When Tampa Bay reassigned Pena to Minor League camp, it would have been natural for the once-promising prospect to ponder another line of work, or at least to look for a Big League job with another club.

Instead, Pena extended his hand to Manager Joe Maddon and said, "Thank you very much for the opportunity. I will be back."

Indeed he was — by Opening Day because of an injury to Norton. Pena ended up being named the American League Comeback Player of the Year in 2007 with 46 home runs, 121 RBI and 103 walks.

"You can't focus on the magnitude of what's at stake," said Pena, who was eventually rewarded with a three-year contract with the Rays. "Otherwise you'll drive yourself crazy. But there's no doubt that the last week of Spring Training is a tough time for a lot of guys in the clubhouse."

Not only can the roster moves made in week six of Spring Training determine the fate of a season, they also can change careers — and lives. Familiar with comeback stories like Pena's, general managers are afraid of turning away a player that comes back to haunt them by making contributions elsewhere. Many general managers almost hope for a minor injury on the roster late in March that will allow them to keep an additional player for at least a few weeks.

"There are a lot of factors involved," said Jim Bowden, former general manager for the Washington Nationals and Cincinnati Reds. "You're preparing for a 162-game marathon, not a 30-game sprint. Whether or not a player has options is a factor. It's not just about performance in March."

"Some guys are just a victim of numbers," said Reds Manager Dusty Baker. "But usually guys will distinguish themselves or delete themselves. I'm just the guy who tells them."

Japanese hurler Hideo Nomo put together 11 successful Major League seasons after arriving on the scene with the Dodgers in 1995. He won 12 or more games seven times, but that resume still didn't help him make the White Sox's roster in Spring Training of 2006. He was assigned to Triple-A Charlotte, and ultimately was released by Chicago in June.

Sometimes it can be difficult to re-assign a player — literally. Former Diamondbacks Manager Bob Melvin recalled when he was serving as the club's bench coach in 2001, and he — along with Manager Bob Brenly and hitting coach Dwayne Murphy — had to inform first baseman Erubiel Durazo that he was being sent

COMING AND GOING

Young baseball prospects have much to offer their organizations — talent, versatility, a fresh outlook for the season. But they're also valuable for another less discussed reason — they've got options.

A player is said to be on optional assignment if he is named to a team's 40-man roster, but is not on its active roster. The days following Spring Training are prime for placing athletes on optional assignment because, although a multitude of non-roster players are invited to camp, only 25 are chosen for a slot on the active roster come April. The rest must either be released or assigned.

Major League ballplayers are given three options to be exercised during the first three years of their careers, meaning that they may be transferred between their club's Major League squad and Minor League affiliates as many times as the team desires during that time. After spending more than 20 days in the Minors during any one of these years, a player exhausts one of his options.

Optional assignments expire when a player from the 40-man roster has spent more than 20 days in three seasons in the Minor Leagues. Once a player is out of options, he must either be placed on his team's active roster or placed on waivers to be claimed by another club.

Veteran athletes may refuse their options once they have accrued more than five years of Major League experience. Those who refuse an option to the Minors are granted free agency. However, if an athlete has fewer than five years of experience in the Big Leagues, a club may send him down to the Minors for a fourth year without subjecting him to waivers.

down despite a terrific spring. Upon hearing the news, Durazo, who was in utter disbelief, wouldn't budge from Brenly's office.

"Murphy, Brenly and I are looking at each other thinking, 'He's not going anywhere. What do we do now?'" Melvin recalled. "Finally Dwayne got up and said, 'Ruby, we have to go talk,' and he responded to that."

Durazo would return and play a key role for the 2001 World Series champions, belting five pinch-hit home runs and launching 12 longballs overall in 175 at-bats.

"He was right; he deserved to make the team," Melvin said. "But there are some guys who come to camp and no matter what they do, they're not going to make the team because of people already there. After that spring he had, there wasn't much more he could do to prove himself. Fortunately, once the season starts, it's not long before a spot opens up."

TUNNEL VISION Players work tirelessly to refine their game right up until the end of Spring Training.

KNOTHOLE A young Seattle Mariners fan catches a glimpse of his favorite club working out during Spring Training.

PLEASE
KEEP OFF
THE FENCE

ROOM AND A VIEW
While fans are still
relaxed late in Spring
Training, it's a tense
time for many players.

ALL ABOARD After a six-week Spring Training that is both strenuous and relaxing, stressful and leisurely, it's time for the A's to return to Oakland and get the 2001 regular season started.

BIBLIOGRAPHY

Pregame

Page 13: Ave, Melanie and Curtis Kruger. "Remembering Al Lang: St. Petersburg's Mr. Baseball." *The St. Petersburg Times*. March 23, 2008.

Page 13: Fountain, Charles. *Under the March Sun*. New York, N.Y.: Oxford University Press, 2009.

Page 14: Veeck, Bill with Ed Linn. *Veeck as in Wreck*. New York, N.Y.: G.P. Putnam's Sons. 1962. p. 176-182.

Week 1

Page 19: Topkin, Marc. "Tampa Bay Rays Pack Heavy for Move to New Spring Facility." *The St. Petersburg Times*. Feb. 8, 2009.

Page 28: Williams, Pete. "The 'A' Team. Under New Skipper Tony La Russa, St. Louis Unleashes The 'A' Team." *USA Today Baseball Weekly*. February 21-27, 1996. p. 4-6.

Week 2

Page 46: Jenkins, Chris. "Blooming Cactus League Quenches Desert Thirst." *The San Diego Union-Tribune*. Feb. 10, 2009.

Page 62: Appel, Marty. *Slide Kelly Slide*. Lanham, Md.: Scarecrow Press. 1996.

Page 62: Byrd, Alan. *Florida Spring Training: Your Guide to Touring the Grapefruit League*. Branford, Conn.; The Intrepid Traveler, 2004.

Page 62: Williams, Pete. "In Pursuit of a Signature." *USA Today Baseball Weekly*. May 15-21, 1996. p. 32-34.

Week 3

Page 70: Armida, Gary. "Pitching Perspectives with Rick Peterson: Inside Spring Training." FullCountPitch.com. March 2, 2009.

Page 70: Romano, John. "Tampa Bay Rays Keep a Tight Rein on Their Starting Pitchers." *The St. Petersburg Times*. March 2, 2009.

Page 73: Bowman, Mark. "Smoltz Catches up with Ex-teammates." MLB.com. March 30, 2009.

Page 73: Fountain, Charles. "St. Patrick's Day is Spring Training's Big Holiday." *The Boston Globe*. March 17, 2009.

Page 73: Langosch, Jenifer. "Bay Reminisces as Bucs Visit." MLB.com. Feb. 26, 2009.

Page 73: Zolecki, Todd. "Burrell relishes reunion with Phillies." MLB.com. Feb. 28, 2009.

Page 76: Pearlman, Jeff. "Spring Training is Just One Part of Lou Brock's Wonderful Life." SI.com. March 3, 2009.

Page 81: Fountain, Charles. "St. Patrick's Day is Spring Training's Big Holiday." *The Boston Globe*. March 17, 2009.

Page 84: "Selleck No Hit at Bat In Cameo Appearance." The Associated Press. April 4, 1991.

Page 84: "Yankees release Billy Crystal on 60th birthday." The Associated Press. March 14, 2008.

Week 4

Page 98: Kaspriske, Ron. "Let's Play Two: The Twin Passions of Baseball and Golf are a Hit at Spring Training." *Golf Digest* Feb. 2002.

Page 98: Peterson, Erik. "Atlanta Braves Rebuild on the Diamond, Remain Strong on the Golf Course." GolfChannel.com. March 8, 2009.

Page 108: Byrd, Alan. "Amusement Perks." *Street & Smith's Pro Magazine*. Summer 2001. p. 25-26.

Week 5

Page 133: Johnston, Joey. "Lopez Field Was a Memorable Place." *The Tampa Tribune*. May 5, 2009.

Page 139: Olney, Buster. "Pinstriped for Greatness." *The New York Times*. March 21, 1999.

Page 139: Williams, Pete. "The Seattle Sound: Mariners Set to Rock the A.L. with their '97 North American Tour." *USA Today Baseball Weekly*. April 2-8, 2007. p. 28-30.

Week 6

Page 142: Williams, Pete. "Survival of the Fittest." *Major League Baseball 2001: The Official Guide to the 2001 Season*. Major League Baseball Properties, Spring 2001, p. 66-72.

CREDITS

CHARLES FRANKLIN/MLB PHOTOS: Cover, 130-131
J. MERIC/GETTY IMAGES: Back cover, 71, 78-79, 84-85
OZZIE SWEET: Back cover, 94-95
GEORGE SILK/TIME LIFE PICTURES/GETTY IMAGES: Back cover, 44-45, 96-97
MARK CUNNINGHAM/MLB PHOTOS: Back cover, 22, 29, 30-31, 82-83, 89

BRAD MANGIN/MLB PHOTOS: 2-3, 120-121, 140
WALTER IOOSS JR./SPORTS ILLUSTRATED/GETTY IMAGES: 5, 91
RICH PILLING/MLB PHOTOS: 6, 50-51, 56-57, 58, 60, 62-63, 74-75, 104-105, 107, 112, 134-135, 136, 137
LOUIS DeLUCA/MLB PHOTOS: 8
ST. PETERSBURG MUSEUM OF HISTORY: 10

VANGUARD PUBLICATIONS: 12, 14-15
SF GIANTS/MLB PHOTOS: 16, 26-27, 48-49, 100-101
FPG/GETTY IMAGES: 18
MISSY MIKULECKY/SF GIANTS/MLB PHOTOS: 20-21
ELIOT J. SCHECHTER/GETTY IMAGES: 23, 138
ELSA/GETTY IMAGES: 24-25

MICHAEL ZAGARIS/MLB PHOTOS: 32-33, 90, 154-155

TONY FIRRIOLO/MLB PHOTOS: 35

STEPHEN DUNN/GETTY IMAGES: 36-37, 87, 118

RON VESELY/MLB PHOTOS: 38, 64-55, 86

JASON WISE/MLB PHOTOS: 40-41, 42, 43, 54-55

KIRK SCHLEA/MLB PHOTOS: 47

RONALD MARTINEZ/GETTY IMAGES: 52

JEFF CARLICK/MLB PHOTOS: 59

DOUG BENC/GETTY IMAGES: 66-67, 68, 80

MICHAEL IVINS/MLB PHOTOS: 72-73

DAVE ARRIGO/MLB PHOTOS: 77, 106

LA DODGERS/MLB PHOTOS: 81

FERNANDO MEDINA/NBAE/GETTY IMAGES: 92

RONALD C. MODRA/SPORTS IMAGERY/GETTY IMAGES: 99

COURTESY OF DON & CHARLIE'S: 102

CHRISTIAN PETERSEN/GETTY IMAGES: 103, 126-127, 147

JON SOOHOO/MLB PHOTOS: 108, 116

DOUG PENSINGER/GETTY IMAGES: 109

AL MESSERSCHMIDT/GETTY IMAGES: 110-111, 114-115

RICK STEWART/GETTY IMAGES: 122-123

JONATHAN WILLEY/MLB PHOTOS: 124-125, 150-151, 153

DIAMOND IMAGES/GETTY IMAGES: 128

BRIAN BAHR/GETTY IMAGES: 129

CHICAGO WHITE SOX/MLB PHOTOS: 132-133

DAVID SEELIG/GETTY IMAGES: 143

ETHAN MILLER/GETTY IMAGES: 144-145

BRUCE WEAVER/AFP/GETTY IMAGES: 148

BEN VANHOUTEN/MLB PHOTOS: 152

INDEX

Al Lang Field, 10-11, 13, 50-51, 107, 131

Al Lopez Field, 9, 46, 113, 132-133

Al Lopez Park, 113

Alomar, Roberto, 53

American Academy of Dermatology, 88

Anaheim Angels, 53

Anson, Cap, 11

Appel, Marty, 62

Arias, George, 84

Arizona Biltmore Resort & Spas, 104

Arizona Diamondbacks, 9, 14, 34, 46, 56-57, 104, 124-126, 131, 149

Arizona State University, 76

Asadoorian, Ricky, 42

Associated Press, The, 53

Athletes' Performance Institute (API), 40-43

Atlanta Braves, 12, 28, 52, 57, 73, 88, 98, 108-109, 113, 119, 133

Auerbach, Red, 81

Baker, Dusty, 149

Baldelli, Rocco, 73

Baltimore Orioles, 11-12, 14, 46, 52, 113, 139, 146

Barajas, Rod, 131

Baseball City, Fla., 9, 34, 133

Bass, Kevin, 84

Bay, Jason, 73

Beckett, Josh, 95

Bell, George, 139

Bell Road (Arizona), 46

Beltran, Carlos, 62-63

Bench, Johnny, 133

Berman, Chris, 133

Bern's Steakhouse, 107

Berra, Yogi, 9, 69, 76, 84, 96-97

Billingsley, Chad, 138-139

Black, Bud, 76

Boggs, Wade, 133

Boston Beaneaters, 62

Boston Braves, 13

Boston Celtics, 81

Boston College, 57

Boston Red Sox, 12, 23, 40, 52, 57, 64-65, 70, 72-73, 79, 81, 95, 113, 126, 141

Bowden, Jim, 149

Bradenton, Fla., 12, 62, 76-77, 107, 113

Bradenton Beach, Fla., 106

Brenly, Bob, 149

Brett, George, 34, 69, 76, 133

Bright House Networks Field, 52, 110

Brock, Lou, 76

Brooklyn Dodgers, 13, 81 also see Los Angeles Dodgers

Brooks, Garth, 87

Buckley, Jay, 52, 113

Burrell, Pat, 40, 73, 107

Busch Gardens, 107, 133

Caladesi Island Beach, 107

Camelback Mountain, 104

Camelback Ranch, 9, 46

Campanella, Roy, 134

Canseco, Jose, 53

Carlson, Mark, 84

Casa Grande, Arizona, 100

Catalina Island, Ca., 14, 104

Celebration Golf Club, 98

Chamberlain, Joba, 92-93

Champion Stadium, 52, 108

Charleston RiverDogs, 36

Charleston, S.C., 11

Charlotte Sports Park, 19, 52, 95

Chase Field, 104

Cheesecake Factory, 46

Chicago Bulls, 87

Chicago Cubs, 9, 14, 35, 37, 46, 103, 119, 126, 141, 145

Chicago White Sox, 14, 46, 84, 86, 113, 133, 141, 148-149

Chicago White Stockings, 11

Cincinnati Redlegs, 133

Cincinnati Reds, 9, 12, 14, 46, 52, 81, 84, 107, 113, 133, 149

City of Palms Park, 52

Clark, Tony, 139

Clearwater Beach, 61, 107

Clearwater, Fla., 12, 73, 76, 88, 107, 110, 131

Cleveland Indians, 14, 46, 102

Collins, Terry, 84

Colorado Rockies, 14, 34, 46

Conine, Jeff, 139

Costello, Chris, 19

Cox, Bobby, 88, 98, 108, 119

Crawford, Carl, 40

Creek, Doug, 95

Crisp, Coco, 28

Crystal, Billy, 69, 84-85

Curtis Fundamental Elementary School, 110-111

Dale Mabry Highway, 113

Daulton, Darren, 88

Davenport, Fla., 133

Davis, Eric, 139

Deer, Rob, 84

Derby Lane, 107

Desert Botanical Garden, 104

Detroit Tigers, 9, 12-13, 22, 29-31, 34, 38-39, 52, 57, 76, 82-84, 89, 107, 113, 139

DiMaggio, Joe, 13

Disney's Wide World of Sports, 28, 52, 73, 88, 98, 108-109

Disney World, 9, 12, 93, 107-108, 113, 133

Doby, Larry, 14

Dodgertown, 13, 46, 52, 62, 81, 134-137

Don & Charlie's Steakhouse, 61, 102, 104, 113

Doug Creek Charters, 95

Duckworth, Brandon, 146-147

Duncan, Kathy, 110

Dunedin, Fla., 12, 88, 107, 110, 131

Dunedin Stadium, 52, 62, 107, 110-111

Durazo, Erubiel, 149

Dykstra, Lenny, 88

Ebbets Field, 134

Eckersley, Dennis, 22, 28, 126

Ed Smith Stadium, 52

Eiland, Dave, 146

Erickson, Scott, 139

ESPN, 133

Fielder, Cecil, 139

Florida Aquarium, 107

Florida Marlins, 12, 34, 46, 52, 57, 146

Florida's First Big League Baseball Players, 13

Florida Southern College, 57

Florida State League, 110, 133

Florida Strawberry Festival, 107

Floyd, Cliff, 28, 76, 88

Ford, Whitey, 94-95

Fort DeSoto Park North Beach, 107

Fort Lauderdale, Fla., 12-13, 46, 139

Fort Lauderdale Stadium, 52

Fort Myers, Fla., 12, 23, 95

Fountain, Charles, 11, 81

FOX Sports, 53

Francoeur, Jeff, 98

Frank Lloyd Wright Foundation, 104

French Lick, Indiana, 104

Frenchy's Restaurant, 61

Gagne, Eric, 139

Gainey Ranch, 104

Gallego, Mike, 28

Garciaparra, Nomar, 40, 73, 75, 126, 139

Garvey, Steve, 133

Geddes, Norman Bel, 134

Gehrig, Lou, 13, 197

George M. Steinbrenner Field, 9, 43, 52, 84, 113-115

Geren, Bob, 139

Getty Images, 53

Giambi, Jason, 28, 46, 126-127

Gibson, Bob, 76

Gibson, Kirk, 139

Giles, Brian, 57

Ginn Reunion Resort, 98

Girardi, Joe, 88

Glavine, Tom, 28, 88, 98

Glendale, Ariz., 14, 46

Gooden, Dwight, 133

Goodyear, Ariz., 14, 102

Goodyear Ballpark, 9, 14, 46

Gossage, Rich "Goose," 126

Grand Canyon, The, 46, 104

Granderson, Curtis, 29

Grim, Bob, 94-95

Gross, Gabe, 28

Guidry, Ron, 76

Gwynn, Tony, 62, 87-88

Hairston, Jerry, 43

Halicki, Ed, 26-27

Halladay, Roy, 88

Hammond Stadium, 52

Hanke, C. William, 88

Hanlon, Ned, 11

Hatcher, Mickey, 76

Hatteberg, Scott, 54

Hayhurst, Dirk, 28

Heard Museum, 104

Henderson, Rickey, 43, 126, 130

Henley Field, 13

Hernandez, Livan, 70

Hi Corbett Field, 14, 46

Hodges, Gil, 134

Hoffman, Trevor, 88

Hohokam Park, 46, 104

Holman, Bud, 134

Holman Stadium, 13, 134, 137

Hornsby, Bruce, 69, 84

Hot Springs, Ark., 11

Houston Astros, 12, 22, 52, 61-62

Houston Chronicle, 61

Hubbell, Carl, 100-101

Hudler, Rex, 142-143

Hudson, Orlando, 139

Hurricane Restaurant, 107

Innisbrook Resort & Country Club, 107

Isleworth Golf & Country Club, 98

Isringhausen, Jason, 95

Jack Russell Stadium, 110

Jackson, Bo, 133

Jackson, Reggie, 9, 76, 84

Jacksonville, Fla., 11, 13

Jay Buckley's Baseball Tours, 52, 112-115

Jenkins, Ferguson, 70, 126

Jesuit High School, 113

Jeter, Derek, 40, 84, 139

Jockety, Walt, 28

Johnson, Randy, 119, 131

Joker Marchant Stadium, 13, 29, 52, 57, 84, 113

Jones, Adam, 40

Jones, Chipper, 28, 88, 98, 108

Jordan, Michael, 84, 86

Joyner, Wally, 87

Jupiter, Fla., 12, 25, 34, 46, 76

Justice, Richard, 61

Kaline, Al, 9, 69, 76

Kansas City Royals, 14, 28, 46, 76, 87, 133, 146

Kansas State University, 76

Kapler, Gabe, 28

Kelly, Mike "King," 62

Kent, Jeff, 139

Kissimmee, Fla., 12, 52, 61-62

Kotchman, Casey, 52

Koufax, Sandy, 9, 69, 76, 134

Kruk, John, 88

Laird, Gerald, 22

Lakeland, Fla., 9, 12-13, 22, 29, 31, 57, 76, 84, 107, 113, 139

LaMar, Chuck, 146

Lang, Al, 9, 13

Lankford, Ray, 43

LaRoche, Adam, 98

La Russa, Tony, 28, 43

Lasorda, Tommy, 134

Las Vegas, Nev., 141, 145

Layana, Tim, 84

Leatherman, Stephen ("Dr. Beach"), 107

Lee County, Fla., 12

Leesburg, Fla., 13

Liriano, Francisco, 70-71

Litsch, Jesse, 131

Little League Baseball Challenger
    Division, 87
Lockhart, Keith, 118
Lodwick School of Aeronautics, 13
Longoria, Evan, 146
Lopez, Al, 113, 133
Los Angeles Angels, 14, 46-47,
    52, 62, 84, 142
Los Angeles Coliseum, 141
Los Angeles Dodgers, 9, 14, 40, 46, 52,
    62, 76, 117, 134-139, 141, 149 *also
    see* Brooklyn Dodgers
Lowe, Derek, 135, 139
Lowry Park Zoo, 107
Lutz, Fla., 107
Maddon, Joe, 57, 70, 149
Maddux, Greg, 88, 98
Magadan, Dave, 113
Maholm, Paul, 84
Mantle, Mickey, 13, 94-95
Marchant, Marcus "Joker," 13
Martin, Billy, 94-95, 126
Maryvale, Ariz., 14, 102
Maryvale Stadium, 46
Marzano, John, 139
Mattingly, Don, 76, 139
Mays, Willie, 76
Mazeroski, Bill, 76-77
McCovey, Willie, 76
McGee, Willie, 28
McGowan, Dustin, 119
McGraw, Tug, 81
McGriff, Fred, 9, 133
McKechnie Field, 52, 62, 113
Meche, Gil, 70
Melvin, Bob, 131, 149
Merloni, Lou, 43
Mesa, Ariz., 14, 102, 104
Milwaukee Brewers, 14, 28, 46
Minnesota Twins, 12, 34, 52, 70, 95,
    113, 126
Minoso, Minnie, 133
Mr. Baseball (movie), 84
Mitchell, Bo, 87
MLB Network, 9
MLB Photos, 53
MLB Players Association, 88
Moffitt Cancer Center, 88
Molitor, Paul, 99
Montreal Expos, 53, 76, 146
Morneau, Justin, 40
Mota, Manny, 136
Murphy, Dwayne, 149
Naimoli, Vince, 57

National Basketball Association
    (NBA), 81, 87
National Football League (NFL), 34,
    113, 119, 133
Nelson, Jeff, 57
NESN, 22
New Orleans, La., 11, 13
New York Giants, 13-14 *also see* San Fran-
    cisco Giants
New York Mets, 12-13, 28, 36, 46, 50,
    52, 57, 62-63, 67, 70, 76, 87, 91
New York Yankees, 12-13, 28, 36, 40,
    43, 46, 52, 53, 57, 76, 84-85, 88,
    94-95, 104, 107, 110, 113-115,
    139, 146
Nicklaus, Jack, 98
Nomo, Hideo, 148-149
Norton, Greg, 149
Oakland Athletics, 14, 28, 32-33, 43,
    46, 54, 62, 70, 126, 139, 154
O'Malley, Walter, 13, 81
Ordonez, Rey, 113
Orlando, Fla., 52, 98, 107, 113, 133
Orlando Magic, 93
Orlando Rays, 108
Osceola County Stadium, 52, 61, 62
Outdoor Channel, The, 95
Palmer, Arnold, 98
Palm Harbor, Fla., 107
Patterson, Dwight, 14
Paul, Chris, 87
Pedroia, Dustin, 40, 79
Pena, Carlos, 28, 149
Peoria, Ariz., 14, 87, 102, 139
Peoria Sports Complex, 9, 14, 46, 76, 88
Percival, Troy, 88, 95, 119
Pesky, Johnny, 78-79
Peters, Chris, 113
Peterson, Rick, 70
P.F. Chang's, 46
PGA Champions Tour, 98
PGA Tour Children's Miracle
    Network Classic, 98
Philadelphia Phillies, 12-13, 34, 46,
    52, 73, 76, 81, 88, 107, 110,
    143, 146
Phoenician, The, 104
Phoenix, Ariz., 13-14, 34, 46, 48,
    57, 102-104
Phoenix Art Museum, 104
Phoenix Municipal Stadium, 14, 28,
    32-33, 46, 62
Phoenix Zoo, 104
Piniella, Lou, 60, 113, 119, 133

Pink Pony Restaurant, 113
Pittsburgh Pirates, 12, 52, 73, 76, 84, 107
Plant City, Fla., 107
Players Choice Awards, 108
Play Sun Smart (skin cancer awareness), 88
Pompano Beach, Fla., 126
Port Charlotte, Fla., 12, 19, 46, 57
Port St. Lucie, Fla., 12, 46, 76, 87
Posner Park, 133
Price, David, 70, 146
Puckett, Kirby, 126
Pujols, Albert, 87
Punta Gorda, Fla., 95
Radke, Brad, 95, 113
Raines, Tim, 146
Ramirez, Manny, 40
Raymond James Stadium, 113, 133
Riley, Roger, 34
Ripken, Cal, 43, 139
Riske, David, 58
Riske, Payton, 58
Roberts, Brian, 40-41, 139
Robinson, Jackie, 134
Rodriguez, Alex, 84, 139
Roenicke, Ron, 76
Roger Dean Stadium, 9, 25, 34, 52
Rose, Pete, 133
Rothschild, Larry, 57
Ruppert, Jake, 13
Ruth, Babe, 13, 18, 107
Ruth, Dorothy, 18
Ruth, Helen, 18
Ryan, Nolan, 69-70, 76
St. Louis Cardinals, 12, 24-25, 28, 34,
    43, 46, 50, 52, 57, 87, 131
St. Louis University, 57
St. Patrick's Day, 68-69, 80-83
St. Pete Beach, Fla., 107
St. Petersburg, Fla., 9, 13, 19, 28, 43,
    46, 50, 57, 91, 107, 131
Sanchez, Freddy, 40
San Diego Padres, 14, 28, 46, 53, 57, 76,
    87, 126, 130, 146
San Francisco Giants, 9, 14, 16-17, 20-
    21, 26-27, 35, 37, 46, 48-49, 62,
    100-101, 126 *also see* New York Giants
Santana, Johan, 67
Sarasota, Fla., 12, 14, 84, 133
Savannah, Ga., 11
Schilling, Curt, 40, 88
Schmidt, Mike, 69, 76
Schuerholz, John, 133
Scioscia, Mike, 76
Scottsdale, Ariz., 14, 61, 102, 104, 112-113

Scottsdale Stadium, 46, 62, 113
Seattle Mariners, 14, 46, 117, 139, 141, 145, 152
SeaWorld, 108
Sedona, Ariz., 46, 104-105
Sele, Aaron, 138-139
Selig, Bud, 88
Selleck, Tom, 84
Sheffield, Gary, 133
Shouse, Brian, 28
Singletary, Wes, 13
*61 (movie), 84
Slide, Kelly, Slide, 62
Smoltz, John, 28, 72-73, 88, 98
Sorenstam, Annika, 98
Space Coast Stadium, 35, 52
Steinbrenner, George, 57
Stenhouse, Jay, 53
Stevens, John, 133
Stewart, Dave, 126
Stoneham, Horace, 14
Stottlemyre, Todd, 28
Surhoff, B.J., 139
Surprise, Ariz., 14, 102
Surprise Stadium, 9, 46, 76
Taliesin West, 104
Tampa, Fla., 9, 12-13, 43, 57, 76, 107, 113, 132-133, 146
Tampa Bay Buccaneers, 113, 133
Tampa Bay Rays, 12, 19, 28, 36, 46, 50, 52, 53, 57, 70, 73, 88, 95, 108, 110, 131, 146
Tampa Tarpons, 133

Tarpon of Boca, 95
Tarpon Springs, Fla., 107
TBS, 22
Teammates for Kids Foundation, 87
Tempe, Ariz., 14, 40-43, 52, 76, 102
Tempe Diablo Stadium, 46-47, 62, 120-121
Texas Rangers, 14, 46, 70, 76, 126
Thomas, Frank, 62
Thomson, Bobby, 13
Tiger Town, 13
Toma, George, 34
Toronto Blue Jays, 12, 28, 46, 52, 53, 62, 88, 107, 110, 119, 131, 139, 142
Torre, Joe, 46, 52, 57, 76
Touch 'em All Foundation, 87
Towers, Kevin, 46, 76, 87, 126, 130
TPC Tampa Bay, 107
Tradition Field, 52
Tropicana Field, 19, 107, 131
Tucson, Ariz., 14, 34, 46, 57, 102, 113, 124-125
Tucson Electric Park, 46, 56, 126
Under the March Sun, 11, 81
Universal Studios, 108
University of Georgia, 57
University of Miami, 57
Varitek, Jason, 74-75
Veeck as in Wreck, 14
Veeck, Bill, 9, 14, 102
Vero Beach, Fla., 9, 13, 52, 62, 76, 134
Verstegen, Mark, 42

Viera, Fla., 12
Wade, Ed, 22
Waechter, Doug, 131
Washington Nationals, 12, 35, 52, 149
Washington Senators, 11, 13
Watson, Tom, 98
Wells, Vernon, 40, 88, 110
Westmoreland, Chris, 19
West Palm Beach, Fla., 76, 88, 98
Whitaker, Lou, 139
White, Frank, 76, 133
Whitt, Ernie, 139
Williams, Mike, 36
Williams, Mitch, 88
Williams, Robin, 84
Wilpon, Fred, 76
Wilson, Willie, 133
Winfield, Dave, 69, 76, 139
Winter Haven, Fla., 9, 14
Woods, Tiger, 73, 98
World Baseball Classic, 28, 108
Wright, David, 87
Wright, Frank Lloyd, 104
Wrigley Field, 14
Ybor City, Fla., 107
Youkilis, Kevin, 40-41, 87
Yount, Robin, 99
Yuma, Ariz., 14
Yuma Country Club, 139
Zaun, Gregg, 142
Zimmer, Don, 140-141
Zito, Barry, 90